MAY I ANSWER THAT?

Sri Swami Sivananda

Published by

THE DIVINE LIFE SOCIETY

P.O. SHIVANANDANAGAR—249 192

Distt. Tehri-Garhwal, Uttaranchal, Himalayas, India

Price] 2006 [Rs. 90/-

First Edition:	1992
Second Edition:	1994
Third Edition:	1999
Fourth Edition:	2006

[2,000 Copies]

©The Divine Life Trust Society

ISBN 81-7052-104-1

ES 101

Published by Swami Vimalananda for
The Divine Life Society, Shivanandanagar, and printed by him at
the Yoga-Vedanta Forest Academy Press,
P.O. Shivanandanagar, Distt. Tehri-Garhwal, Uttaranchal,
Himalayas, India

SRI SWAMI SIVANANDA

Born on the 8th September, 1887, in the illustrious family of Sage Appayya Dikshitar and several other renowned saints and savants, Sri Swami Sivananda had a natural flair for a life devoted to the study and practice of Vedanta. Added to this was an inborn eagerness to serve all and an innate feeling of unity with all mankind.

His passion for service drew him to the medical career; and soon he gravitated to where he thought that his service was most needed. Malaya claimed him. He had earlier been editing a health journal and wrote extensively on health problems. He discovered that people needed right knowledge most of all; dissemination of that knowledge he espoused as his own mission.

It was divine dispensation and the blessing of God upon mankind that the doctor of body and mind renounced his career and took to a life of renunciation to qualify for ministering to the soul of man. He settled down at Rishikesh in 1924, practised intense austerities and shone as a great Yogi, saint, sage and Jivanmukta.

In 1932 Swami Sivananda started the Sivanandashram. In 1936 was born The Divine Life Society. In 1948 the Yoga-Vedanta Forest Academy was organised. Dissemination of spiritual knowledge and training of people in Yoga and Vedanta were their aim and object. In 1950 Swamiji undertook a lightning tour of India and Ceylon. In 1953 Swamiji convened a 'World Parliament of Religions'. Swamiji is the author of over 300 volumes and has disciples all over the world, belonging to all nationalities, religions and creeds. To read Swamiji's works is to drink at the Fountain of Wisdom Supreme. On 14th July, 1963 Swamiji entered Mahasamadhi.

1

Why should we believe in God?

Belief in God is an indispensable requisite for every human being. It is a *sine qua non*. Owing to the force of Avidya or ignorance, pain appears as pleasure. The world is full of miseries, troubles, difficulties and tribulations. The world is a ball of fire. The Antahkarana charged with Raga, Dvesha, anger and jealousy is a blazing furnace. We have to free ourselves from birth, death, old age, disease and grief. This can be done only by faith in God. There is no other way. Money and power cannot give us real happiness. Even if we exercise suzerainty over the whole world, we cannot be free from care, worry, anxiety, fear, disappointment, etc. It is only faith in God and the consequent God-realisation through meditation that can give us real, eternal happiness and free us from all kinds of fear and worries which torment us at every moment. Faith in God will force us to think of Him constantly and to meditate on Him and will eventually lead us on to God-realisation.

2

What is the harm in not believing in God's existence?

If we have no faith in God, we will be born again in this world and will undergo considerable miseries. The ignorant, faithless doubting self goes to destruction. He cannot enjoy the least happiness. Neither this world nor that beyond is there for the doubting self. Those who have no faith in God do not know what is right and what is wrong. They have lost the power of discrimination. They are untruthful, proud and egoistic. They are given to excessive greed, wrath and lust. They hoard up money by unlawful means. They become men of demoniacal nature. They commit various sorts of atrocious crimes. They have no ideals for their lives. They are thrown into demoniacal wombs. They sink into the lowest depths, deluded birth after birth.

Some one hundred and fifty years ago there lived a very famous Yogi-jnani by name Sadasiva Brahmendra Sarasvati in Nerur, near Karur, in the district of Tiruchirapalli in South India. He is the author of *Brahma Sutra Vritti* and *Atma Vidya Vilasa* and various other books. He has done innumerable miracles. Once when he was absorbed in Samadhi on the banks of the Cauvery, he was carried away by the flood and thrown somewhere else. He was deeply buried underneath the sand. Labourers went to plough the fields. They hit against the head of the Yogi and some blood oozed out. They dug out, and to their great astonishment, they found a Yogi seated in Samadhi.

On another occasion, as an Avadhuta, Sadasiva Brahmendra entered the Zenana of a Mohammedan chief naked. The chief was quite enraged at the sage. He cut off one of the arms of the Mahatma. Sadasiva Brahman walked away without uttering a word and without showing any sign of pain. The chief was greatly astonished at this strange condition of the sage. He thought that this man must be a Mahatma, a superhuman being. He repented much and followed the sage to apologize. Sadasiva never knew that his arm was cut off. When the chief narrated to the sage what had happened in the camp, Sadasiva excused the chief and simply touched his maimed arm. Sadasiva Brahman had a fresh arm. It is the life of this sage that made a very deep impression in my mind. I came to a very definite conclusion that there is a sublime divine life independent of objects and the play of the mind and the senses. The sage was quite unconscious of the world. He did not feel a bit when his arm was cut off. He ought to have been absorbed in the Divine Consciousness, he ought to have been one with the Divine. Ordinary people yell out when there is even a pin-prick in their bodies. When I heard of the marvellous incident in the life of Sage Sadasiva from Apta persons and when I read in the book, it gave me a very strong conviction about the Divine Existence and a divine eternal life where all sorrows melt, where all desires are satisfied and one gets supreme bliss, supreme peace and supreme knowledge.

3

What is Brahmamuhurta? Why is it eulogised by the Rishis?

4 a.m. in the morning is termed as Brahmamuhurta. Because it is favourable for meditation on God or Brahman, it is called Brahmamuhurta. At this particular hour, the mind is very calm and serene. It is free from worldly thoughts, worries and anxieties. The mind is like a blank sheet of paper and comparatively free from worldly Samskaras. It can be very easily moulded at this time before worldly distractions enter the mind. Further, the atmosphere also is charged with more Sattva at this particular time. There is no bustle and noise outside.

4

What is your opinion of the Masters of the Himalayas?

There is a great Master of Masters, the Indweller of your heart. Turn the gaze inwards, withdraw the Indriyas and seek His help. Rest in Him. Identify yourself with Him. Search Him in your heart. Don't talk to me of these Himalayan Masters in future. You will be deluded.

5

What is the difference between Japa and meditation?

Japa is silent repetition of the Name of the Lord. Meditation is the constant flow of one idea of God. When you repeat *Om Namo Narayanaya,* it is Japa of the Vishnu Mantra. When you think of the conch, disc, mace and lotus flower in the hands of Vishnu, His ear-rings, the crown on His head, His yellow silken Pitambar, etc., it is meditation. When you think of the attributes of God such as omniscience, omnipotence, etc., it is also meditation.

6

The Lord's grace will do everything for me. Why should I do any Sadhana?

This is wrong philosophy. God helps those who help themselves. God's grace will descend only on those persons who exert. The Lord's grace will descend in proportion to the degree of surrender. The more the surrender, the more the grace. You cannot expect the Lord to do self-surrender for you. Be up and doing.

Strive. Plod. Persevere. The Lord will shower His grace upon you.

Mira abandoned everything. She renounced kingdom, husband, relatives, friends and property. She remembered her Lord Krishna whole day and night. She shed tears of Prem. She sang His praise with single-minded devotion. She gave up food. Her body got emaciated. Her mind was ever absorbed in Lord Krishna. Only then did Lord Krishna shower His grace upon her.

7

Give me a very simple, but very impressive proof for the existence of the soul.

You say in daily life, "My body", "My Prana", "My mind", "My Indriya". This clearly denotes that the Self or Atman is entirely different from the body, the mind, the Prana and the Indriyas. The mind and the body are your servants or instruments. They are as much outside of you as these towels, chairs, cups are. You are holding the body just as you are holding a long walking stick in your hand. You are the possessor or proprietor of this body. The body is your property or possession. The body, the senses, the mind, etc., are not the soul, but belong to it.

8

If God is beyond the reach of the senses, He should be a non-entity, a mere void, a negative concept, a metaphysical abstraction. Something beyond the senses? How could this be? I cannot believe such things. I am a scientist. I want accurate laboratory proofs.

You want laboratory proofs? Very fine indeed! You wish to limit the illimitable all-pervading God in your test-tube, blowpipe and chemicals. God is the source for your chemicals. He is the substratum for your atoms, electrons and molecules. Without Him no atom or electron will move. He is the Inner Ruler, Antaryamin. He is the Niyanta. Without Him the fire cannot burn, the sun cannot shine, the air cannot move. Without Him you cannot see, cannot talk, cannot hear, cannot think. He is the maker of all scientific laws, the law of gravitation, the law of cohesion, the law of attraction and repulsion, etc. He is the law-giver. Bow to Him with faith and devotion. You will have a thorough knowledge of the Science of sciences, Brahma Vidya, through His grace and you will attain Moksha.

9
Why do Sadhaks fail to realise God quickly nowadays?

After attaining a certain stage of development, they begin to dissipate their energies in preaching, in making disciples, in publishing books. They become the slaves of name and fame. That is the reason why they fail to reach the highest goal of life, viz., Brahma Sakshatkar.

10
How can Kundalini be awakened? Would Japa alone be successful in awakening the Kundalini?

Kundalini can be awakened by the practice of Asan, Pranayam, Mudras, Japa and by the grace of a Guru. Refer to my book "Kundalini Yoga".

Yes. Japa alone is quite sufficient to awaken the Kundalini. There is no doubt of this. Sri Samarth Ramdas awakened the Kundalini by doing Japa of the Mantra *Om Sri Ram Jaya Ram, Jaya Jaya Ram* thirteen crores of times by standing in the river Godavari, in Takli Village, near Nasik.

11

What are the three Doshas or faults in the mind? Give a concrete illustration.

They are Mala or impurities such as lust, anger and greed, Vikshepa or tossing of the mind or mental oscillation, and Avarana or the veil of ignorance.

There is a muddy lake covered with moss. The wind is blowing hard. Now, the lake is the mind. The muddy condition represents Mala. The agitation of the waters that is set up by the wind corresponds to the Vikshepa in the mind set up by the vibration of Prana. The moss that covers the surface of the water represents the veil of ignorance.

12

How to make the mind subtle and pure?

Do Japa. Do selfless service. Pray to God from the bottom of your heart (Antarika). Have Satsang. Meditate. Read the Gita and the Upanishads. Live alone. Live in seclusion for six months. Take Sattvic food. Give up meat, fish, eggs, liquors, chillies, oil, black sugar, onions and garlic.

13

What is the difference between Bhakti and Jnana?

Bhakti is devotion. It is a means to the end which is attainment of Jnana. People of emotional temperament are fit for this path. It demands self-surrender or Atma-nivedan. It is the cat-Yoga. The kitten cries aloud and the mother cat runs at once to catch it by the mouth. So also, the devotee cries aloud like Draupadi and Gajendra and the Lord Krishna runs immediately to rescue him and shower His grace. The Bhakti Marga demands only sincere, intense devotion, blind faith and strong conviction as Prahlad had. There is no necessity for learning. Illiterate people like Tukaram who could not sign even their names had realised God. There is no need for vast learning or study. A Bhakta wants to eat sugar-candy. He wants to sit by the side of the Lord.

Jnana is the Yoga of self-expansion. It demands self-reliance. Only people of an intellectual temperament with Vichara Sakti or the power of discrimination and ratiocination are fit for the path of Jnana or knowledge. It is the monkey-Yoga. The young monkey does not cry, but itself clings tenaciously to the body of its mother wherever the mother runs. This Yoga demands a vast study of Vedantic literature, a sharp intellect, bold understanding, gigantic will and courage. A Jnani wants to become an embodiment of sugar-candy, instead of tasting sugar-candy. A Jnani wants to become identical with the Existence (Eka Aikyam).

14

Are Jnana and Bhakti conflicting with each other?

My answer is emphatically "No". There is, in fact, an inter-relationship between these two, the one supplementing the other. Bhakti is not at all antagonistic to Jnana. There is undoubtedly a mutual dependence between the two. Both lead to the same destination.

You cannot entirely separate Bhakti from Jnana. When Bhakti matures, it becomes transmuted into Jnana. A real Jnani is a devotee of Lord Hari, Lord Krishna, Lord Rama, Lord Siva, Durga, Sarasvati, Lakshmi, Lord Jesus and Buddha. He is a Samarasa Bhakta. Some ignorant people think that a Jnani is a dry man and has no devotion. This is a sad mistake. A Jnani has a very, very large heart. Go through the hymns of Sri Sankaracharya and try to gauge the depth of his devotion. Go through the writings of Sri Appayya Dikshitar and measure the magnanimous depths of his unbounded devotion.

Swami Ram Tirth was a Jnani. Was he not a Bhakta of Lord Krishna? If a Vedantin excludes Bhakti, remember he has not really grasped and understood Vedanta. The same Nirguna Brahman manifests with a little Maya in a corner as Saguna Brahman for the pious worship of His devotees.

Bhakti is not divorced from Jnana. On the contrary, Jnana intensifies Bhakti. He who has a knowledge of Vedanta is well established in his devotion. He is steady and firm. Some ignorant people say that if a Bhakta studies Vedanta, he will lose his devotion. This is wrong. Study of Vedanta is an auxiliary to increase and develop one's devotion. The devotion of a man proficient in Vedantic literature is well-grounded. Bhakti and Jnana are like the two wings of a bird to help one to fly unto Brahman, to the summit of Mukti.

15

Is it advisable to do meditation after meal at night? A Grihastha is so much disturbed in the evening that he scarcely gets time to meditate.

After a sumptuous meal, generally, people feel drowsy. You may imagine that you are meditating, but it may be purely sleep in a sitting posture. If you follow the rules of Mitahara and take meals before 7 p.m., you can sit and meditate from 9 p.m. to 10 p. m.

Meditation at night, a second sitting, is absolutely necessary. If you do not have sufficient time at night, you can meditate even for a few minutes, say, ten or fifteen, before going to bed. By so doing, the spiritual Samskaras will increase. The spiritual Samskaras are valuable assets or priceless treasures for you. Further, you will have no bad dreams at night. The divine thoughts will be carried during sleep. The good impressions will be there.

16

I find it very difficult to keep up Brahmacharya. Suddenly I fall in the pit foolishly. Actually I am crying, but doing the same act like a dog. What is to be done?

Fast. Do Japa of a Mantra for three hours daily. Read the Gita, one chapter daily. Sleep in a separate room. Keep the mind fully occupied. Divert the mind. Entertain noble, sublime thoughts. Have Satsang. Do simple Pranayam with mild Kumbhaks twenty times daily. Do a lot of physical work also. Take simple food.

Think that there is neither sex nor sexual Vasana in Atma. Meditate on Atma.

17

I am in earnest search of a Guru who can emphatically say that he has realised Brahman or the eternal Truth or God. Can you give trace of such a man? May I take the liberty to ask you whether you have realised Brahman?

The queries you have asked are quite common to all sincere aspirants in the spiritual path.

Suppose I tell you that a certain "X" is a realised soul, how can you verify my statement and how far will you be benefited by him?

Realised souls are not rare. Ordinary ignorant-minded persons cannot easily recognize them. Only a few persons who are pure and are embodiments of all virtuous qualities can understand realised souls and they only will be benefited by their company.

There is no use of running hither and thither in search of realised men. Even if Lord Krishna remains with you, He cannot do anything for you, unless you are fit to receive Him. Realise this point well and purify yourself by Nishkama Karma Yoga, charity, concentration, meditation, Japa, Brahmacharya and control of senses.

Testing a Guru is highly difficult. Don't use your intellect here. Have faith. The real aspirant is quite free from such questions and doubts. You will be miraculously helped if you believe in my words.

18

Is it too much for a teacher to make his followers great?

The question assumes that the teacher has *attachment* for his disciple in preference to others. If he had that, he would not be a spiritual teacher, because the first qualification for a spiritual man is conquest of attachment. The fact is that out of millions, one is found to have the qualification and it is he who comes up as 'the great'—the superman. Each such great man is surrounded by men who are attracted by his inherent charm. But those who are so surrounding are not the people who are qualified to be masters. They are just ordinary men and no more.

19

A rather unusual lady studied for ten years under the strictest Yogic discipline with some of the "greatest of all great Yogis" and finally came to the conclusion....that it is all a hoax and a mirage.

From your account of her, she was not qualified to benefit by contact with anyone, even if that one had the spiritual greatness of Lord Buddha himself. The one thing needed for spiritual progress is *perseverance*. She was stuffing herself with the writings of many, each of whom pointed a different path. One who wants to sink a well must go on digging in one place till one strikes water. If he digs pits in a hundred places, each not more than 5 feet deep, he will not have dug a well. That was her case. What value can be attached to her opinions?

20

Why is so much sanctity attached to a pilgrimage, and not to a mere sight-seeing trip or an official tour?

It is because the very idea of "going on a pilgrimage" prepares your mind to be in a highly receptive mood, in a highly prayerful mood. It shuts out the worldly grooves in the mind. You leave the cloak of your official life in your office room. You abandon the cumbersome apparel of social life when you leave your town or city. Even if you travel with your family, you gradually begin to look upon the family members as co-pilgrims and not so much as personal relations. If you are alone, perhaps you live completely in a spiritual world of your own, with little or no family cares, worries and anxieties. This is the mental condition that is most conducive to the greatest reception of the spiritual vibrations that surround you on all sides in holy regions like Uttarakhand. The pilgrim who goes as a pilgrim is conscious that he is engaged upon a sacred mission of gathering spiritual impressions and will therefore gain the greatest blessings by a pilgrimage. He will be a thoroughly changed man when he returns from the Yatra.

21

How are people benefited by a pilgrimage?

This question has to be answered by each pilgrim for himself. The spiritual benefit always depends entirely upon the heart's faith. Faith is the life-breath of the spirit in man. No spiritual endeavour can be fruitful without it. With it, no spiritual achievement is impossible. If a pilgrim heartily believed, was convinced, and was certain-at-heart that all his sins would be washed away, that he would attain Moksha and get beyond the wheel of Samsara, there is absolutely no reason why it should not actually prove to be so. A pilgrimage like Badri-Yatra can wash off all your sins and enable you to take great strides towards the Great Goal—Self-realisation—if you have firm faith in its glory. But, remember, the test of this faith is what you are after you return from the pilgrimage; if, after the pilgrimage, you prove that you have been thoroughly purged of all your sins, that all the evil Samskaras have been washed away by the holy waters of the rivers you have bathed in, and that you have been filled with the spiritual vibrations of the sublime atmosphere you have sojourned in, and if you live a pure life of righteousness, devotion, truth, love and purity, you have certainly been liberated. The pilgrimage has served its supreme purpose.

Some pilgrims do rise to such spiritual heights, though their number may be small, and though they may not advertise their achievements.

22

I read your article in "My Magazine": "Fly from the company of worldly-minded persons. Those who talk of worldly affairs will pollute you. Your mind will waver. Run, run, run quickly to solitary places like Rishikesh. You will be safe in the spiritual path". May I come to you and lead the life of a Sannyasin?

Do not be hasty. Think well. Look before you leap. Mere emotion will not do in the spiritual line. The above instructions are for those who were already doing some kind of Sadhana. They will have to go in for seclusion for advanced practices. It will be better for beginners like you to perform Nishkama Karma Yoga for three years in the world by disinterestedly serving the sick and the aged persons.

Suppose you remain with me as a Sannyasin, have you got the real strength of heart to face your mother when she weeps bitterly before you with a broken heart? Will you stick to this line if your father comes and threatens you? Will you be unaffected in your mind if a young lady tempts you? Will you be steady if you are affected by a disease? Are you prepared to sacrifice this body and life in the cause of Truth? Have you understood the glory and importance of Sannyasa and seclusion? Have you got an idea of the difficulties that Sannyasins have to face? Are you prepared to go from door to door and live on Bhiksha? How will you spend the whole day and night when you live in seclusion? Just decide all these points before you come to me. If you are sure that you are fit for Sannyasa, you can come here. I will serve you and help you well. I will take care of your spiritual welfare. I will make you a king of kings. There is nothing so pleasant, as the life of renunciation. It is best suited for quick Self-realisation. Glory to all Sannyasins!

23

Why should I—the Brahman, I—the Cosmic Consciousness, the Existence without another, the Infinite, the All-pervading and the Omniscient, at all project Prakriti? Why must I be bound by the laws of Prakriti and be limited by the phenomena of time, space,

causation and substance, and above all, why must I get involved in this process of evolution and involution?

The eye cannot perceive itself. A man cannot stand on his own shoulders. Even so, all enquiry into the Ultimate Cause, the causeless Cause of all creation, is first confronted with a formidable wall of primordial ignorance. He who annihilates his ego to nothing at this point, and who thus obtains the grace of Isvara, gets through this wall and enters the Kingdom of the Infinite. Then he *knows*. But this knowledge cannot be communicated to others, as this great wall is obstructing others from perceiving the Truth. Therefore the ancient sage termed it an Ati-prasna or transcendental question.

Suffice it to know that God has created this world in order to enable you to evolve and realise the Self, in order to serve all and love all as His manifestations. The dacoit of ignorance has kidnapped man from his palace of Self-awareness and brought him to a thick forest; when the man wakes up, he does not brood over how he came there, but tries to get out of the forest. Even so, the earnest Sadhak tries to break the chain of transmigration by attaining Self-realisation.

24

Why does not the benevolent, kind and all-merciful God help the righteous man and give him happiness? Why does He leave him to the mercies of his Purva Karma?

Karma is likened to the wheel. It has to work out; because the force that set it in motion has to be spent. It is a cycle of action and reaction. Just as the arrow once discharged from the bow cannot be withdrawn, even if the hunter feels that he has aimed at a wrong target, Prarabdha Karma, the fruit of those Karmas performed in previous births that have come up for experience in this present birth, cannot be annulled.

How then does God help His devotee? The all-merciful God does help His devotee by strengthening his will-power, his power of endurance, to bear the Karma-Phala with a cheerful countenance. The devotee is certainly not left to the mercy of his Purva Karma; he is beautifully clothed in the protective shield of His grace. Just as in the worst winter and violent storm, you remain unaffected in your own house and in your warm clothing, the devotee (though to the onlookers he is poor, sick or suffering) does not feel that he is suffering at all and is ever happy and blissful in His remembrance.

25

A man doing a wrong thing argues that he is doing it because of his Karma; and he does not even try not to do it, because it gives him immediate happiness. How to impress upon him not to do it?

Karma does not compel a man to do wrong actions. Samskara does, to a certain extent. But God has bestowed free will on man, with which to make or mar his career. Man has no Bhoga-Svatantrata or the freedom to enjoy or suffer, which factor is governed by Karma. But, he has got Karma-Svatantrata or freedom to do good or evil. He can substitute good Samskaras in place of the old vicious Samskaras by Vichara-sakti, will-power and continued practice of good actions.

That evil seems to give immediate happiness is the greatest temptation and the greatest obstacle to the cultivation of virtues; and it can be removed only by discrimination and experience. Contemplation over the ultimate and permanent damage done to the very soul of man by the evil actions, and the harm he is causing to the entire society itself by his evil, ought to compel a man to desist from evil action—however pleasant it might appear superficially. There is no short-cut to this really serious problem; the wicked heart will not yield easily. And therefore our ancients have exalted Satsang. Constant association with the wise and spiritually evolved persons alone can remove these wrong notions from the mind of the wicked one.

26

I am a stranger whom you would never have dreamt of coming across, but please do not detest me for being a woman. I am only too eager to taste the happiness of spiritual life. Please, Swamiji, have some consideration even for a woman and tell me whether I am to be blessed with such happiness in my future, and if so, when that will be.

It is said that one must have a proper Guru and I do not know where to hunt for one who would satisfy my appetite soon. Can you help me?

Did you yourself have a Guru and who was he? Tell me all about him, please, if I am not being too bold in asking this. Is he, or was he, a Satguru?

May I know whether you can be called a Guru or a Satguru?

I am extremely pleased to note that you are too eager to taste the happiness of spiritual life. You have good spiritual Samskaras. Protect them. You can realise that spiritual happiness through regular practices.

I do not detest anybody. I revere a woman as my own Self. Woman is a manifestation of Sakti. I adore her as Durga or Mother Kali. Though ladies are styled as Abalas (those without strength), they are dynamic forces on this earth. Religion is maintained through them alone. The devotional element is ingrained in Hindu ladies. They have innate devotion. If they determine, they can realise God very quickly.

Don't you like to become a Mira? If your mind is really turned towards God-realisation, if you are sincere and earnest in your spiritual practices, you will attain the spiritual bliss in a short time. Cheer yourself up. Be bold. Stand up. Assert. Recognize. Realise. Taste the spiritual happiness.

You can find your Guru at your door if you really want him. Sincere aspirants are rare. Yes, I have my Guru. Space will not permit here to tell all about him. I am neither a Guru nor a Satguru. I take great delight in serving others. Surely I shall serve you and share with you whatever I have. I shall clear your doubts, put you in the spiritual path.

27

Is it dangerous to practise Pranayam without the assistance of a Guru or teacher?

You can practise ordinary Pranayam exercises without the help of a Guru. There is no danger in practising Pranayam, Asan, etc., if you are careful, if you use your common-sense. People are unnecessarily alarmed. There is danger in everything if you are careless. If you are careless in getting down the steps of a staircase, you will fall down and break your legs. If you are careless when you walk in the busy parts of a city, you will be crushed by the motor-cars. If you are careless when you purchase a ticket at the railway station, you will lose your money-purse. If you are careless in dispensing mixtures, you will kill the patients by giving a poison or a wrong medicine or by administering a medicine in over-doses. Even so, when you practise Pranayam, you will have to be careful about your diet. You should avoid over-loading, you should take light, easily digestible and nutritious food. You should be moderate in copulation. You should not go beyond your capacity in retaining the breath. You should first practise inhalation and exhalation only (without retention of breath) for one or two months. You should gradually increase the ratio from 1:4:2 to 16:64:32. You should exhale very very slowly. If these rules are observed, there is no danger at all in the practice of Pranayam.

A Guru is necessary if you want to practise Kumbhak or retention of breath for a long time and unite Apana with Prana. The books written by realised Yogins can guide you if you are not able to get a Guru. But it is better to have a Guru by your side. Or you can get the lessons from him and practise them at home. You can keep regular correspondence with him. You can retain the breath from ½ to 1 or 2 minutes without any difficulty or danger. If you cannot get a realised Yogi, you can approach senior students of Yoga. They also can help you.

28

Does purity of food lead to purity of mind? Is non-vegetarian food not Sattvic? We have in the Mahabharata instances of people taking the meat of goats sacrificed to the Lord.

Yes, purity of food leads to purity of mind. *Aharasuddhau Satvasuddhih.* Take a dose of champagne and sit for meditation. Take a dose of orange-juice and sit for meditation. You will know the difference. Different foods exercise different influences on different compartments in the brain. By taking champagne, meat and garlic, the mind will be confused and will become restless when you sit for meditation. By taking milk and fruits, you will get good concentration. Our Rishis lived on fruits and milk. The Chhandogya Upanishad says, "Pure food leads to purity of mind and then one attains Moksha". You should have dietetic discipline.

Non-vegetarian food is not Sattvic. It is not good for a seeker. Live for a month on milk and fruits and see. Give up meat for one month and see. Let us be practical. Practical experience will tell you that meat-eating is bad for the mind.

29

Which is better? To lead a family life or to become a recluse?

You cannot renounce the world all at once. The world is a vast university. Nature is the best teacher. In the world you can develop virtues like mercy, tolerance, etc. You cannot develop them if you remain in a cave. The world is the best teacher. Gradually, when you have evolved, you can renounce. Guru Nanak remained in the world with two or three children. There is nothing wrong in the world. Prayer will remove all obstacles.

30

It is rumoured in certain quarters that friendship with Sadhus and Sannyasins can do and undo the well-being of a person. If a person hurts the feelings of some God-realised saint, then it is said that the saint may curse and thus herald a bundle of miseries for him. How far is this true?

The company of Sadhus and Sannyasins is always covetable provided they are of sterling character. If this singular qualification is traceable in them, they are worthy of adoration and respect. They can never be a source of trouble to anyone.

Contact with Sadhus and Sannyasins of true worth can never mar the progress or the personal interests of people. The Sadhus help people to mould themselves on right ethical principles. Their blessings are an invaluable asset to the latter. Satsang with Sadhus and Sannyasins overhauls the vicious Samskaras that the worldly-minded people are naturally prone to.

A God-realised saint never curses others even though he is provoked to the extreme, but simply prays to the Almighty—not to protect him from dangers or save him from dishonour, but to bestow Jnana, light, purity and illumination on his opponents. He never hurts others even though he is hurt. He simply forgives and forgets. He remains oblivious of any wrong done to him. A true God-realised saint finds his own beloved Deity in the thief, the debauchee, the rogue, the murderer, the assailant, the ant, the dog, the Pariah, the Brahmin, the tree, the stone, the scorpion, in fact, in the entire living and non-living creation. He is at-one with all. When such is the case, when he sees his own Self everywhere, whom can he curse?

Remember that a Sadhu or a Sannyasin is not God-realised if he curses others for any reason. It is true that the curse of any pious man, not necessarily a Sadhu or a Sannyasin, readily acts on the person towards whom it is directed under pressure of mental hurt or physical harm.

31
When the grace of Guru and God is there, why is the mind still not controlled?

There must be Purushartha also. Only when you do Purushartha, the grace will come. A professor will not answer the questions for you and make you pass. The Gita says, *"Uddharet Atmanatmanam"*. One should raise oneself. Grace only helps one to raise oneself. Everybody should work out his own salvation. You may ask, "What is grace then?". If an aspirant gets letters from his preceptor, clearing his doubts, that is grace. If an aspirant comes here, takes Ganges bath and hears the lectures here, that is grace. Many people are thirsting, even *croropathis* (those who possess crores of rupees) are thirsting to come and bathe in the Ganges, but all do not get a chance of coming and having their wish fulfilled. If good books are available for Svadhyaya (study), it is grace. If one enjoys good health for doing Sadhana, that is grace. If God so wishes, He can give Mukti to the whole world in an instant; but He does not do so. Grace descends only when there is Purushartha.

32

Why has God created the world?

Ask God why He has created this world! Attain wisdom of the Self. Then you will know why God created the world. You cannot understand it with your intellect. You can understand it only with intuition.

For the sake of sport, God created the world. *Lokavattu Lila Kaivalyam.* Creation of the world has a purpose. Just as we cannot have a sun without rays, similarly, we cannot have God without the world process. The world is like His rays. It is His Svabhava, nature. Just as a juggler produces something and makes it disappear, so also, God produces this world and makes it disappear. God is omnipotent. To ask why He created the world is an Ati-prasna, a transcendental question. We will be only wasting time by discussing it. Before asking about the world, ask about yourself. Know who you are. Then you will know everything.

33

Is there a remedy for the fall of ethical laws and standards due to the industrial revolution?

The industrial revolution does not compel anyone to lower the moral standard. No doubt, it might have facilitated this fall to some extent. The real mischief was done by the misleaders of mankind who deliberately exalted material values over spiritual values. It is never too late to mend. Even now, if the heart of man be cleansed of the dross of selfishness and self-aggrandizement, and righteousness enthroned in it, the moral standard can be kept high in spite of the most spectacular industrial development.

34

Why does man not remember death and cease forthwith from sinful deeds keeping the transience of earthly life in view?

Every man has not sprung up all on a sudden as a man. The Jiva, right from the very first ushering into the world, continues to undergo the cycle of births and deaths not in tens, hundreds or thousands, but in lakhs. It actually carries with it the Samskaras right from its very first birth up to the birth current, i.e., under enjoyment. The unenjoyed or residual Samskaras continue till they are completely fried in toto by Atma Jnana. The very forgetfulness of death by man, though he sees countless deaths daily, indicates the nescience that has developed in him to avoid seeing the face of Truth. The experiences that he has gained thus far, i.e., up to the moment of consideration, are quite insufficient to drag his attention towards the eternal truth which is God. A day will certainly dawn in the life of every individual on this earth, not necessarily in this very birth itself, when he will, by some rare merit, through Satsang with Mahatmas, devotion to Guru, or God's grace, tune in to the Ultimate by gradual evolution.

The sinful deeds which men commit are mainly due to ignorance. When ignorance vanishes once and for all by performance of good and selfless deeds, Japa, Svadhyaya, etc., or by Guru Kripa, the final goal ever remains in view. Commission of vicious deeds indicates that the Jiva is not yet an evolved one and that he is to gain more and more experiences of the world and undergo repeated and continual refinement from grossness. For the disappearance of ignorance and firm remembrance of God, there is no way more powerful than to encounter the kicks, blows and knocks of the world that may greet one unawares.

35

What standards should be adopted to measure true greatness?

The true greatness of man is to be measured not by the amount of wealth nor by the number of bungalows which are had nor by the exercise of personal influence, but by the degree of selflessness, all-embracive outlook, generosity, liberal views, cosmic benefaction, self-sacrifice, egoless, self-effacing nature, grade of perception of unity in diversity, humanitarian services, etc. A truly great man is pious, spiritually elevated, magnanimous and noble-hearted. He can never have a thought for himself and he ever prefers the welfare of humanity casting aside all petty, selfish and personal interests. He ever prays for the welfare of humanity. Where there is an open, unconstricted, expansive and large heart, there lies true greatness.

36

Who is a righteous man?

A righteous man is he who is pure in thought, word and deed and who observes Yama and Niyama to the very letter. He ever sticks to Dharma even in the face of a bayonet. He never moves astray for the sake of paltry gains and selfish ends. He is ever pious, God-fearing, Self-centered and selfless. He has cosmic vision and a broad outlook. He is equanimous and tolerant towards all. He is a mine of all virtues like charity, nobility, sincerity, humility, renunciation, serenity, simplicity and so on. No egoism, no lust, no greed, no crooked-mindedness, no vanity can find a place in him. The righteous man is ever the object of adoration to all. There will be no enemies to him at all, for he loves all friends and foes equally.

37

How can a person perpetuate the period of youth?

The Yogic method excels all other methods. It is the best and the cheapest of all prevalent systems of treatment. Take to intense Pranayam and Asans. Both these help a lot in preserving Veerya (semen) and converting the vital energy into Ojas. Practise Sirshasan, Sarvangasan, Matsyasan, Halasan, Paschimottanasan, Padahastasan and Yoga Mudra coupled with Bhastrik Pranayam. Practise Pranayam till the stage of Kevala Kumbhak is reached. When there is no necessity either to breathe in or to breathe out, Veerya becomes steady; that is, there will be no discharge or emission in any form. The Ayurvedic preparation "Chyavanaprash" is a wonderful one in enabling the regular user to preserve youth for a very long time.

38

In an article in "Siva's Treasure" entitled, "Are you really qualified?", you write under Para III, "If a thing is refused to him (the Sadhak), he should not aspire for it again". Does this statement not advocate a false sense of self-satisfaction and defeatist mentality? Please reconcile the discrepancy and oblige.

"If a thing is refused to him (the Sadhak), he should not aspire for it again."

Read this statement again and again till it suffuses your entire being, till the proper substance of it is totally realised by yourself. Then only you will appreciate the grand truth to imbibe its true spirit. *"Neither ask nor reject"* should be the motto of an ideal Sadhak. He should not have any special craving for any particular object, however dearest and cherished it be. Whatever comes by chance *without any self-effort* can be had, provided that it does not degrade the individual from the moral standards. He should not develop any attachment to any object lest he should suffer mentally when the object is weaned away from him or refused to him by the will of the Lord. Everything comes and goes as per His sweet will. Whether one strives for an object or not, when something is due, it certainly befalls to one's lot of its own accord. Aspirants should cultivate mental detachment and indifference towards good and evil, happiness and misery, love and hatred and all sorts of pairs of opposites. Such mental equanimity can be acquired by Atma-Vichara (self-enquiry), study of sacred scriptures, Satsang with Mahatmas, etc. Self-sacrifice, self-contentment and self-denial are what are required in the spiritual field for progress. It is no defeatist mentality if the Sadhak rests satisfied with his ordained lot without yielding himself even mentally to the temptations which he previously used to enjoy. He is certainly not the "fox that remarked that the grapes were sour when he could not reach to have them". By voluntary self-denial and dispassion or by keeping equanimity when something pleasing does not fall to one's share, tremendous will-power accumulates. It is therefore a necessity to keep balance of mind in all states of working consciousness.

39

What is Nadi Suddhi in its technical sense? How to feel that one has attained perfect Nadi Suddhi?

Nadi Suddhi means purification of the nerves (Nadis). Nerve is not the correct English term for Nadi. There is no appropriate word for Nadi in English.

Complete fast, preferably without any liquid or solid food, practice of Asans and Pranayam, and intense physical exercise—all go a long way in the elimination of fat and other unwanted matters and in the overhauling of the system to confer the benefit of Nadi Suddhi. Asans and Pranayam can purify the nerves, if done with the correct technique.

When one attains Nadi Suddhi, the body becomes light. Stool becomes scanty. There is agility in movement and activity in demeanour. No trace of slothfulness or indolence can be detected. While walking, the body appears to be floating in the air. The tone of the voice changes from hoarseness or gruffness to mellifluence. Hopping, jumping and dancing while at work can be observed in one endowed with Nadi Suddhi. Something inexpressible forces the person to do this and to achieve something grand in his lifetime.

40

What are the best and the worst methods to retaliate against a wrong done to us for no fault of ours?

Whether a wrong is done on some basis or not, it is not to be retaliated against in any way if one wants real moral and spiritual strength and the Lord's grace. Calmly bear the wrong done to you without the slightest mental upset or loss of psychic equilibrium. Do good to the man that does harm. Bless that man that curses you. Pray for the well-being of the man that beleaguers you. Study the lives of Jaya Deva, Shams Tabriez, Jesus Christ, Gauranga and other saints. The Lord Himself protects His devotees if they surrender themselves totally unto Him, pouring forth prayers unto Him like Draupadi or Gajendra. Do not degrade yourself by resorting to retaliation in any way. Adherence to violence even in thought just to satisfy the lower mind debases the individual spiritually.

The best method to retaliate against a wrong done without any reasonable ground is by way of offering a spiritual treatise like the Gita or the Ramayana to the opponent and praying for his gaining the knowledge of the Self and avoiding the evil ways which are due to his ignorance of the essential unity of all creation. Observe silence and indifference with heart-moving prayers unto the Lord.

41

Does the mental equilibrium of an advanced Yogi get affected when attacked by some serious disease? How does he react on such occasions?

Never. If there is any thought of the body or the disease or the bodily affliction or something that cannot be tolerated by the fleshy frame, remember that he is no advanced Yogi or saint or Sannyasin. He who has no thought of himself or the surroundings or the world, he who is centered in his own Self or his beloved Ishta Devata or gracious Guru, and he who is entirely oblivious of limitations of any sort, and identifies himself with the limitless, diseaseless, unconditioned, all-pervasive Brahman, is a true and advanced Yogi or Bhakta or Jnani; and not otherwise.

He can have no match in the whole world in the matter of utter indifference either towards his disease or towards his limited, perishable body or the whole world. He always remains in his own Self and he never loses his balance under any circumstance. He firmly believes that he is the Infinite, the Absolute Brahman. He firmly believes that death awaits all and snatches away everyone at one time or the other and that the six Urmis—Shoka, Moha, Kshut, Pipasa, Jara and Mrityu—are but common to all the Jivas, not necessarily mankind, and that he is the deathless, imperishable and eternal Brahman. Hence there can be no mental upset for him even amidst crucial tests.

42

Was Srimad Bhagavad Gita actually recited by Lord Krishna in the battlefield or is it the imagination of the poet?

Yes. There is no doubt about the Gita having been recited by Lord Krishna in the battlefield. It is not a mere composition of Chiranjivi (eternally living) Vyasa. Recall to mind the following two Slokas which can be found in the Gita Mahatmya:

Gita Sugeeta Kartavya Kimanyaih Sastravistaraih
Ya Svayam Padmanabhasya Mukhapadmadvinissruta

*Bharatamritasarvasvam Vishnorvaktradvinissrutam
Gitagangodakam Peetva Punarjanma Na Vidyate*

The Gita is not a human composition at all. Have the conviction as such, without the usual questioning intellect. Remember all the Avatara Purushas like Sri Sankara and Sri Ramanuja who had written commentaries on the Gita. Lord Krishna Himself says to one of His lady-devotees named Lilabai that He and the Gita are identical and that worship of the one is adoration of the other. Study Slokas 68 to 71 of the Eighteenth Chapter of the Gita to infuse in yourself the necessary faith and love towards the holy scriptures.

43

Would you kindly suggest some effective methods for conversion and sublimation of the sexual energy into spiritual energy or Ojas?

Observe strict continence in thought, word and deed. Give up thinking useless and vain thoughts. Keep balance of mind in all conditions and circumstances, contemplating the Divine. Practise Sirshasan, Sarvangasan and Oordhva Padmasan, besides Viparitakarani Mudra. Preserve the energy by constantly repeating the Name of the Lord, doing intense Japa and meditation, and study of the Gita, the Bhagavata, the Ramayana and the like. Develop Viveka, Vairagya and Vichara. As dispassion increases, so is the vital energy not allowed to leak out. The greater the Vairagya (non-attachment to worldly objects) the more secure will be the semen. The more the preservation of semen, the greater will be the transmutation into Ojas which means abundant physical, mental, moral and spiritual strength and quick evolution. Pranayam helps a lot in gaining control over the physical machinery and the mind. To have control over the mind means to have control over the Prana Sakti and prevent Veerya from being let out. To have control over this masculine power means to have abundant Ojas which enables the aspirant to glow spiritually. Intense Sadhana, with the desires reduced to the barest minimum, will sublimate the sexual energy into spiritual energy. For further information, go through my book *Practice of Brahmacharya*. It gives exhaustive details regarding the subject in question.

44

Can truth be compromised in the sense that telling a lie is sometimes not only inevitable, but also indispensable? Will such a breaking away from truth be justified?

Truth is truth and falsehood is falsehood. They are as wide apart as the terminals of a diameter of a circle or the north and the south poles. He who wants ethical perfection, who loves Dharma for the sake of the Supreme, *ought to stick to truth* however crucial be the circumstances, however tense be the situation. Think of Harischandra....how he stuck to truth even in the face of trials. How his name is to stand, for all time to come, for truth undimmed! Harischandra was truth personified. That is why he is known as Satya Harischandra. This single instance is enough to sustain man's living on a sound basis of truth, however disastrous and threatening be the crises one has to face. However inevitable and indispensable it be, and however much the situation demands to gain some selfish ends, falsehood should ruthlessly be avoided. Truth and falsehood cannot be linked together. Yoking of the one with the other is awfully absurd. No doubt, in the Bhagavata and other Puranas, a few exceptional instances have been cited, where speaking untruth would be considered appropriate. But they are a matter of exception; they are not applicable to all times and all persons. For illuminating and interesting information in this connection, go through my book, "Ethical Teachings"

45

Due to Prarabdha if a person is to suffer from a disease or if he has to die young, will the repetition of the Maha Mrityunjaya Mantra help him to overcome them?

Prarabdha can be overcome by the grace of the Lord. The Lord's grace descends when there is sincere devotion and when man does Purushartha. Purushartha is possible when the mind is pure. The mind becomes pure when one does acts of kindness and charity. The laws of nature do not operate when there is the grace of the Lord. His grace is all-powerful. We have the instance of Markandeya who conquered death by his Purushartha, by sincere devotion to the Lord. He was destined to die young, but when the Lord's grace descended, Lord Yama had no power to carry out his wish. So it is possible to overcome Prarabdha by *Teevra* Purushartha.

46

Some philosophers lay great emphasis on reason and rational living. What have you to say?

How can reason and logic be given the highest place? The mind, intellect and reason fail when you are under the power of an intoxicant. When anaesthesia is given, where is the logical mind? Does the logical mind function when you have fasted fully for a fortnight? It disappears in sleep and swoon. There are some herbs that incapacitate the mind the moment you take them. Thus, there are many occasions when the logical mind of man becomes impotent and stops its function. How can this logical mind or rational living be given the highest status? Intuition is the highest faculty and the evolution of man is complete when he develops this intuition to the greatest degree and realises his Atman. The knowledge gained in Samadhi is the highest knowledge. It is Samyag-drishti or Tattva-jnana.

47

Of all systems of medicine, which system is the most effective and harmless? Please give reasons.

Every system of medicine has got its own advantages and disadvantages. Each has its own supremacy over the others. Each has its own deficiencies. As regards my view, Ayurveda holds the foremost place in my heart. It has been expounded by Lord Dhanvantari who is the Ayurveda Pita. Ayurveda is the foremost amongst the medical sciences now extant. The effect of its treatment is lasting and unhampered. It is the origin and source of most of the other systems of medicine. As regards immediate cure with the least delay, Allopathy occupies first place in the front rank. Homoeopathy is the most harmless system of medicine and the cheapest in view of cost.

48

I have been trying to do some Sadhana—Japa, meditation, etc.—, but my mind is not concentrated and it gets distracted. I try to control it, but I am not succeeding to a degree of satisfaction. The progress I make is not as good as it ought to be.

You *ought* to have put forth more efforts if you wanted quick progress! Do more of Japa, concentration and meditation. Increase your Vairagya and Abhyasa. At night have Satsang and Kirtan. Do not feel depressed; in due course of time you will make substantial progress. Go on doing little by little.

49

There is such an expression as "the flight of the alone to the Alone". Where is the necessity for a Guru or his grace? God's grace will do, as it is said in the Upanishad.

How will you get God's grace? When you discipline yourself. How will you know how to discipline? By observing others that had walked the path successfully to the goal of perfection. Who are these men who had walked to the goal? It is these that are known as Gurus. So you need their help, their personal example, their encouragement and their grace. Thus, we have come round to the answer that a Guru is necessary as well as his grace. Everything is necessary—Atma Kripa, Guru Kripa and Isvara Kripa.

50

Which is greater—love or wisdom? Bhakti or Jnana?

Keep your intellect in a box. Love and wisdom are one. Bhakti and Jnana are one. Prema leads to Jnana. The one helps the other. People read books and start arguments. Is this great? Or is that great? It is all foolishness. God is both love and wisdom. One should not waste his time in these useless arguments.

51

Swamiji! I live in Lucknow. It is so different from Rishikesh. I would very much miss the calm, peaceful atmosphere of Rishikesh when I go back to Lucknow. The atmosphere there is so artificial. What Sadhana can I do?

Why! You can do wonderful Sadhana there also. The world is not a hindrance. You have got a very practical and thorough knowledge of Vedanta. The fiery spirit of Ram Tirth is in you. Start Brahmamuhurta meditation classes. This is the greatest service you can do to the citizens of Lucknow. Go from Mohalla to Mohalla and preach Vedanta. Open study circles in each Mohalla. Conduct morning Brahmamuhurta meditation classes in each Mohalla by turn. You would be doing a great service to all humanity and to yourself. Awaken people to the real purpose of their life. This would keep your consciousness awake too.

52

Is it possible for a soul with a male body to take a female body in the next incarnation?

O, yes. The soul must undergo various experiences in different bodies. In the male body, the soul experiences the qualities of boldness, strength, etc., and patience, mercy, kindness, forgiveness, etc. in the female body. Moreover, neither a man is a full man nor a woman a full woman. There is woman in man and man in woman also. There are animal traits also in man. There is the dog in some men, there is the donkey in some, there is the jackal in some and the tiger in others. Whichever quality is predominant, the soul takes a body with that particular quality in the next incarnation. Therefore, develop divine qualities. You will evolve quickly and become divinity itself in the end.

53

What is your conclusive opinion about rebirth? Do you really believe that there is rebirth?

What! Having been born a Hindu, and having the blood of the great sages coursing through your veins, do you entertain this doubt in your mind? Yes, undoubtedly there is rebirth.

First of all, you have several miraculous instances of young boys and girls suddenly exhibiting great knowledge. A young girl, who has never studied any book, recites the Gita. How do you account for it except by the fact that she had mastered the Gita in her previous birth, and that by the grace of the Lord, that knowledge has come to the conscious part of her mind in this birth too?

Further, rebirth is a necessity for the soul's evolution. Perfection cannot be achieved in one birth. Even to develop some cardinal virtues it might take several births. If you wish to attain Self-realisation, you have to achieve perfection in all the virtues. You have to achieve perfect self-purification. So, rebirth is a necessity for the Jiva's evolution.

Have you seen the caterpillar moving from one leaf to another? It will reach the edge of one leaf; then project itself; it will catch hold of another leaf, and then only will it entirely leave the first leaf. The Jiva, too, goes about like this. Even before it leaves one body, it has made another (gross or subtle) body according to its Karmas and desires; and it enters this new body with all the Samskaras and Vasanas.

54

What is the interval between death and the next birth? Where does the soul dwell during the period between death and rebirth?

The interval between death and rebirth varies from person to person. It may be two years or it may be two hundred years, or more. There is no hard and fast rule. If the attachment to the world is very intense, a Jiva may be born again immediately after death. There is a girl in Dehra Dun who has memory of her past life. She took her present birth four years after she died in her previous life. Those who have done a lot of virtuous actions remain in heaven for a long time, for two hundred or three hundred years, before they are reborn on earth.

A wicked man will go to another region. You may call it hell. Or it may be a place where he may not get the objects of enjoyment that he wants. A man addicted to drinking may not get liquor there. It may be a place like a jail where one has to break the stones and do such other hard work. But if one has done virtuous deeds, if one is a philanthropist, who has dug public wells, built charitable hospitals, etc., he will go to heaven where he will enjoy for a long time.

55

If the Soul is immortal, why does Swamiji celebrate his birthday which belongs to the body?

I do not celebrate my birthday. It is the devotees who do it. Celebration of such birthdays is equal to worship of Para Brahman. Worship of the Guru is worship of Para Brahman. The devotees take delight in celebrating the birthday, and they are benefited, uplifted. A spiritual wave is created year after year when the birthday is celebrated, and more and more people get a chance of knowing the existence of the Divine Life Society and my teachings. The celebrations of the birthday is an annual reminder to the aspirants of the purpose of their life. It is a fillip to their Sadhana. The pious, receptive attitude prevalent on such an occasion draws forth the grace of the Guru and God upon the devotees. The thoughts of peace, love, devotion, etc., sent out by the innumerable devotees that assemble together to celebrate the birthday go a long way to promote peace, harmony and spiritual well-being in the land.

It is not without purpose that the Hindus celebrate the birthdays of religious leaders, saints and sages, such as Buddha Jayanti, Sankara Jayanti, Mahavira Jayanti, etc. The Hindu calendar is spotted with many such Jayantis and other holy days, so that the observance of these Jayantis and holy days may give the needed spiritual impetus to people and they may strive with increased zeal for the attainment of the purpose of life, viz., God-realisation. The more we have of such special, holy days, the more we have the chance of being inspired to intensify our spiritual progress.

56

When I sit for prayers, the lower mind wanders astray, but the other mind recites the Stotras without the slightest flaw, because of habit. But when I consciously try to recite the prayers, I sometimes miss the link, and have at times to repeat a Stotra from the beginning. Thus, are there two minds? How to overcome this difficulty?

No. There are no two minds. But the mind gets concentration little by little, and the portion of the mind which is spiritually inclined—call it the higher mind—engages itself in Sadhana, whereas that part of the mind which is more aware of its worldly Samskaras runs along its set grooves. Force of habit makes the repetition of prayers mechanical. But the higher mind should be made to concentrate on the meaning. Then the attention of the mind will be held and the lower part of the mind will have less opportunity to detract from the object in view. The whole trouble with careless Sadhana is that it tends to become mechanical without making an impression on the life of the aspirant.

57

Are there fulfilled prophecies in the Hindu scriptures? If so, please explain them.

The Lord has given His ever-standing promise that He would appear on earth whenever there is a danger to

Dharma, whenever Adharma tries to vanquish Dharma. To fulfil that promise He has appeared many times in the form of saints and sages who have protected Dharma from decay and from the onslaughts of foreign oppression. They have instilled new elements of vigour and perspective in Hinduism. Therefore, Hinduism continues to flourish. Whenever there is a necessity, saints and sages will emerge, not from the heavens, but from among the people themselves.

Hinduism does not believe exclusively in one prophet. The prophecies given in the Puranas about the state of affairs to come have also proved true.

58

If I love Jesus, must I love him alone, and not the lesser divinities like Mary and the Ikons?

No. There should be no exclusiveness to the love of Jesus, even though other Christian saints may not be equal to him. They also could be worshipped, if you have devotion for them, as expressions of the same Divinity which manifested itself in a most intense and complete way through Jesus. All messengers of God deserve our respect and adoration. Someone may be temperamentally and emotionally closer to an individual, but it does not mean that the latter should shut the others out. No single prophet or saint holds exclusively the mandate of God or the key to the heavens.

59

I am convinced that praying to saints and worshipping them is absolutely wrong. They prayed to God and found salvation for themselves, and in like manner, we also can take care of our salvation without depending on any saint.

No. It is not so. Saints and sages are worthy of our adoration and prayers, because they have shown us the ways to God-realisation. The apprentice, who has just entered service in any field, is expected to have an attitude of submission and receptivity to his senior who trains him on the job, although the latter may be a man like himself. The same is applicable in the field of spirituality. By respecting saints and following their teachings, you grow in spirituality, you learn to love and know God more adequately.

60

Someone tries to tell me that Nirvikalpa Samadhi is, to quote, "only a strange nerve-condition accompanied by paralysis of the critical faculties". What should I reply, if anything?

It is useless to convince a person about the validity of Nirvikalpa Samadhi when he cannot understand it. Logical arguments may be advanced, but a rank sceptic has to evolve further to be alive to this truth. The philosophical implications and mystic significations of experience must be studied well before one can attempt to answer such sceptics.

61

After one of the most complicated series of dialectics in "The Life Divine", Aurobindo finally concludes with a straight face: "And all these explanations explain nothing". Is there any point, then, any real benefit, in following through the thin thread of this tapestry?

In the ultimate sense, words do not explain Truth. But they give a hint by which one can know Truth directly in experience. Words have a relative value and they must be made use of, though they do not constitute our real aim. Relative obstructions to the knowledge of Truth can be removed through relative means and thus the absolute Truth can be realised.

62

I am under the impression that no advanced Yogi has ever achieved anything in the realm of matter or contributed to progress outside of writing about high, abstract and introspectionist themes and inspiring a small handful to do likewise.

How then do you regard the production of a seemingly supremely great book like Aurobindo's "The Life Divine", which almost nobody reads, almost nobody understands, or books like "Treatise on Cosmic Fire", or your books, all of which seem so totally unrelated to helping anybody individually or collectively, in a material sense?

It is not correct to think that Yogins merely write, but never do anything for human progress. The help that they give, the common man cannot understand, and man has no right to expect a specific form of help from the Yogins, for the Yogins do what is really good and not what is materially convenient to man.

Books which deal with metaphysical subjects and which faithfully explain the goal of life and the method of attaining it are a great help to struggling humanity. Yogins write such books for the good of others, in the spiritual sense and even in a pragmatic sense. But they do something more, too; they give direct, invisible help.

63

How is Kevala Kumbhak done? The practice is not quite clear. It is said to be a Kumbhak without Purak and Rechak. This is not intelligible, for necessarily before the Kumbhak there has to be either inhalation or exhalation.

Your query on the practice of Kevala Kumbhak is not surprising, for it seems to be impossible to do Kumbhak without doing either Purak or Rechak. However, what is meant is that for Kevala Kumbhak the retention is suddenly performed at any given moment when the mind is just about to get concentrated.

This sudden cessation of Prana at that particular, crucial, psychological moment becomes of immense help to the Yogi in arresting the mind, which is already assuming the mood to Dharana. Hence, Kevala Kumbhak is an invaluable aid to Dhyana. You will, therefore, see that this act of Kumbhak is not preceded by any deliberate process of either inhalation (Purak) or exhalation (Rechak). It may, therefore, be best described as the *abrupt stoppage* of the breath. The Yogi *does not deliberately perform* either Purak or Rechak before he does Kevala Kumbhak. He gets into Kevala Kumbhak in whatever state the breathing may be at that moment. It may be in the middle of an inhalation or in the middle of an exhalation. The breath may be partially in or partially out. Or again, the breath may be totally fully inhaled or totally exhaled. Whatever be the condition, the moment concentration supervenes, the meditator immediately arrests his breathing in Kevala Kumbhak. I am sure the matter is perfectly clear now.

64

In my work of spreading the knowledge of Yoga, do you have any special advice to give me?

Side by side with instructions on practical Yogic processes, place always stress upon the great importance of Sadachara, Yama and Niyama. Inspire the students with noble idealism. Spur them on to strive for a life of lofty virtue, active goodness and selflessness. You must stress the need for self-purification and self-mastery. The true inner Yoga is the transformation of the essential nature of man. The lower human nature should gradually give place to an illumined divine nature through a process of spiritualization of the entire being of man. This should be brought home in an effective manner, yet withal with great sympathy, understanding and insight. The aim is to attain divine consciousness.

65

Can prayers cure diseases when doctors fail? Is it true that more things are wrought by prayers than the world could dream of?

Doctors and medicines are only instruments in the hands of God. Unless God wills, none can cure, or get cured. Man should do his best, with initiative, enterprise and perseverance, but depend on God's grace for everything. To bear with suffering and accept it as a blessing of God in disguise is great wisdom. Prayer invokes the inner potentialities of the individual, which flow only from God, and they *can* certainly work miracles.

66

You state that aspirants in the Nivritti Marga should have a little money in the bank or must depend on alms. Now I have no money and I do not like to beg from door to door, but I am very anxious to take Sannyasa. Will you kindly suggest a method to quench my thirst?

There are beautiful Ashrams throughout India where Nishkamya Seva is carried out. They are always in need of sincere and energetic workers. You can remain in any one of the Ashrams and help in the Ashram's activities. They will take care of your material wants. Do not be changing from one Ashram to another. Select the best that suits you and stick to it.

67

I have read that a person, after receiving initiation from one Guru, can, if he finds a better person, become the latter's disciple; and that though he has ceased to be the former's disciple, he should have respect for him also. What is your view?

The vast majority of people do not enjoy the good fortune of coming into contact with a God-realised saint. What happens in their case is this. Traditionally, each family has a Guru-Parampara. Each sect has its own sectional Guru. The aspirant born in a particular sect has, by that mere fact, to accept the Guru of the sect as his own Guru. This Guru is by no means fit to be called so, according to the standards set by our Sastras. He is not a *spiritual* personality, but a religious person. He does not possess Adhyatmic realisation, but is appointed as a religious leader in order not to keep this traditional post vacant. The aspirant takes him as his Guru and receives initiation from him. He practises Sadhana according to his Guru's teachings and up to a certain point he can certainly progress. Up to this point only that Guru himself has gone! To go beyond that stage, that Guru cannot guide the aspirant, because he is not a God-realised sage. At that stage, if the Sadhak happens to meet a Guru of higher achievements, he can certainly become his disciple. In fact, if his first Guru is sincere, he himself will direct the disciple to the feet of another Guru of higher achievements.

If this question of changing the Guru arises in an aspirant who has already received initiation from a Guru who has reached the highest stage, the defect is in the aspirant, not in the Guru. And, even if the aspirant goes to another Guru, this "want" cannot be fulfilled. He must correct the defect in himself and stick to his Guru; he must banish the desire to change his Guru.

Scriptures tell us that if we have once accepted a Brahma-Nishtha as our Guru, we should not change our allegiance to another Guru. The spiritual connection or link is eternal. If an aspirant tries to break it and runs after all kinds of Siddhas and Jnanis, he cannot progress even an inch on the path. The ideal is beautifully stated in the Upanishadic Mantra:

"Yasya Deve Para Bhaktihi Yatha Deve Thatha Gurow
Tasyaite Kathithahyartha Prakasante Mahatmanah"

It means: He who has supreme devotion to God, and as much devotion to his Guru as he has to God, to him the truths of the Upanishads shall be revealed. If devotion to God cannot be changed, devotion to the Guru also cannot be changed.

Do not forget the glorious example of Ekalavya. He did not have even a sight of the Guru; yet, his devotion was so great that he took a mere image to be his living Guru and his Bhavana was so intense that this mud-Guru taught him the great secrets of archery. Here it is Bhavana that really counts.

Upa-Gurus, however, can be countless; this is what the life of the Avadhuta that is narrated in the Bhagavata teaches us. We should respect all saints. The spiritual Guru sows the spiritual seed in us. It is our business to water it, to make it grow in us, so that it might in time yield the delicious fruit of Self-realisation.

68

I desire to reduce my sleeping hours and have control over sleep. Can I take recourse to any medicine?

You should not reduce your sleep by the use of medicine. That will affect your system. Sufficient rest must be given to the body through sleep. When you regularly enter into deep meditation, the system derives considerable rest and automatically sleep can then be reduced. That will not affect your health.

Sleep should be reduced gradually and cautiously. Now, for a month go to bed at 9-30 p.m. and get up at 4 a.m. After a month, go to bed at 10 p.m. and get up at 3-30 a.m. Again, after a month, go to bed at 10-30 p.m. and get up at 3 a.m. Thus, by gradual means you can reduce your sleep. Sleeping in day-time must be avoided.

69

If God is almighty and all-powerful, why can't He see that everybody does his actions properly?

Everybody does his actions properly. A thief must pilfer things. A scoundrel must do wrong actions. These are Kartavya. Remember this world is Trigunatmic and relative. Every movement of the foot, every step, is an attempt towards Sat-chit-ananda. The world is a relative plane. Prostitutes, saints, rogues, beggars, kings are all doing their respective duties. Good and evil are relative terms. Evil exists to glorify good. Hatred exists to glorify love. A rogue is not an eternal rogue. He can become a saint within the twinkling of an eye when he is placed in proper Sattvic company.

70

If God is just and merciful, why should there be so much misery in this world? Sometimes we see virtuous men suffer and hypocrites enjoy. What is the logic in this?

Misery is the eye-opener in this world. Had it not been for the presence of pain and misery, no one would attempt for salvation. Misery is a blessing in disguise.

Virtuous men treat suffering as a blessing as it develops the power of endurance and mercy, and makes them remember God always. They welcome suffering. They do not want worldly pleasure and prosperity. They have a changed vision. They always keep a balanced mind in pleasure and pain. You cannot understand their mental state. They rejoice in suffering. Your mind is still worldly. You cannot understand these things.

71

Equal vision is outlined for Moksha. In this connection, I shall be obliged if you could let me know whether "Don't touchism" has got any significance. I have got too rigid orthodox principles. If I see an untouchable or a sweeper, even from a yard or so, I take a bath and wash my clothes. I shall be glad to know whether these Niyamas should be observed.

Pray to God to give you that day on which you will embrace a scavenger with joy, feeling oneness. That day will be a blessed day. You have a very small, narrow, constricted heart. Try to expand. Slowly give up the "Don't touchism". It will greatly bar your spiritual progress. It will take a long time in your case. You have got a deep-rooted idea of "Don't touchism". In this very second, ruthlessly break all barriers that divide or separate man from man. You will enjoy indescribable joy and supreme peace.

72

When Kundalini is awakened, how to take it to Sahasrara through the various Chakras and how to keep it at a particular Chakra where the Yogi wants it? And how to bring the Kundalini back to Muladhara through the various Chakras? Kindly let me know the movements of the Kundalini.

You will have to take the Kundalini to the Sahasrara Chakra through the practice of Yoni Mudra. If you become absolutely desireless, if the Vasanas are destroyed in toto, Kundalini will ascend by itself without any effort, through the force of purity.

Kundalini will drop down by itself through the force of Prarabdha. It will stop at each Chakra by itself. You need not exert to fix it anywhere. It is better you stay under the proper guidance of a Yogi Guru to learn all these Yogic mysteries and secrets. Try to get ethical perfection before you attempt to awaken the Kundalini and take it to Sahasrara. When you are in the path and when you are sincerely doing Sadhana or Yogic practices, you yourself will know how to take the Kundalini from one Chakra to another. Refer to my book *Kundalini Yoga* for detailed instructions.

73

Is this universe an accidental combination of jarring atoms? Please be kind enough to explain the evolution of the universe.

The universe is not an accidental combination of atoms. The theory of evolution differs according to the different schools of philosophy. The most accepted view, however, is that of the Vedanta. According to it, the universe is a systematic organic whole directed by a supremely intelligent and omnipotent Being behind it. From the relative standpoint, the universe appears as a gradual unfoldment of the primordial matter into the visible gross effects, this matter being actuated by the all-pervading Consciousness Itself. The effects of this matter are, objectively, the five principles of sound, touch, form, taste and smell, giving rise to ether, air, fire, water and earth, and subjectively, the subconscious, the mind, the intellect, the ego, the sense-organs of perception and action, the vital energies and the physical body. All these effects appear as realities, though they are not so actually, because they are based on the one Reality which is the omnipresent Pure Consciousness. From the absolute standpoint, there is no substantial universe at all, except the temporary external form taken by the fluctuating imagination of the mental consciousness within.

74

If an individual is a Perfect Master, he is capable of functioning on all planes at the same time. He possesses to a remarkable degree the powers of clairvoyance and clairaudience. Can he not read the thoughts of the student before the student has time to utter them, before the student can bring out his questions, as Sri Ramakrishna Paramahamsa did? Can one who has such powers, even of thought-reading, be regarded as a Master?

Clairvoyance and clairaudience are not always automatic processes. Unless the Master directs his attention towards someone, he need not necessarily be aware of the seeker's mentality and doubts. Imagine a seer or a Perfect Master who is ever aware of what everybody thinks! A Siddha does see and hear everything in Samadhi. This everything comes then to mean the Self or Atman or Supreme Consciousness where the individual thoughts and words cease to exist as such.

Powers like thought-reading do not necessarily connote perfection; and perfection cannot be vetoed by the absence of these powers. A Perfect Master can acquire these powers if he so wills; but you cannot force him to.

75

What would be your advice to a person who has taken initiation for the second time due to the force of certain circumstances, yet has no faith in the initiator? A compound feeling of attraction and repulsion is the outcome of it. Vascillation between the good principles inculcated from babyhood and the faith as expounded by some now gives rise to a perpetual internal contest. And if the voice of conscience strongly shows disfavour, what would you advise?

Do not mistake your emotions or the promptings of your own mind for the voice of conscience. Only if you have learnt the art of stilling your thoughts for considerable periods of time can you claim to be able to hear the voice of conscience. When you begin to hear it, you will automatically begin following its dictates and all conflicts will end. Vascillation has no antidote except determination, which is so difficult when vascillation is present! You must exercise your will and cut out one of the conflicting thoughts—the one which, according to yourself or the opinion of one whom you are inclined to trust, is the worse.

76

In Kalisantaranopanishad, it is said that repetition of the Maha Mantra is the only means for destroying sins in this Kali Yuga. But this Mantra has two names, Hare Rama and Hare Krishna. As these two names are different, will it not be Vyabicharini Bhakti if the names of two gods are uttered by a devotee? And what is the form to be thought of in meditation while repeating the above Mantra?

It cannot tantamount to Vyabicharini Bhakti. Real Vyabicharini Bhakti is worshipping God for a few minutes and again loving children, wife, property, etc., for the rest of the day. The Supreme Deity behind the two names Rama and Krishna is one. He is Lord Vishnu. For meditation, you can have either the form of Lord Krishna or Lord Rama according to the tendency, predilection or taste of your mind.

77

How do you train your disciples for quick spiritual success?

As a drastic measure to overhaul the vicious worldly Samskaras, I ask the students to drown themselves in active service for some months or years. The period of training varies according to the evolution of the students. They must know cooking, washing, and nursing of the sick. They must serve the Sadhus and the Sannyasins in every possible way. Side by side they must be able to learn all the Yogic exercises, concentration, Japa, meditation, etc. They must be able to write essays on philosophy and Yoga. They must do Kirtan and deliver lectures also. I teach them on all these points. I give them lessons in the treatment of some ordinary diseases. When I find that the students are able to control their senses and advance in concentration and meditation and when I find that they have developed all the Sattvic qualities, I send them to cool places with instructions for deep meditation.

78

I would like to know why we are all created and put to this miserable and pitiable plight. You would

argue that we are never created and never would die. Then why should not we all be in that all-pure, omnipotent state without being entangled by Samskaras and Maya?

Questions like these are Ati-prasnas—transcendental queries—for which you will not get an answer even if you rack your brain for millions of years. Intelligent people leave questions such as the 'why?' and the 'how?' of the universe. If a small son questions his father, "Papa, how did you procreate me?", what answer will Papa give? He will simply say, "Wait. When you become a man, you will understand this point". This is exactly the case with you and several other new aspirants in whom the Light is trying to shine forth. Do not put the cart before the horse. Realise the Atma. Then you will understand these matters. At the present moment, apply yourself to solid Sadhana in earnestness and remove Mala, Vikshepa and Avarana. Do not enter into vain discussions and arguments on such matters. You can ask me questions on other points of philosophy. Wherever you go, you will get the same answer. Have you grasped my point?

79

How can the character of a nation shine forth in its pristine glory?

As far as the Indian nation is concerned, it is essentially spiritual. In olden days, everywhere there used to be Ashrams pulsating with divine ideals and replete with venerable Acharyas who were intensely practical and realised. Even their Sishyas were highly evolved and receptive in their very nature in regard to their Guru's teachings. The degradation in the present era is mainly due to the aping of Western manners and the copying of the Western modes of life without doing even a modicum of justice to how far they are conducive to one's moral, physical, mental and spiritual growth and how far they are helpful in achieving the ultimate perfection known as Moksha which is the be-all and end-all of life. The modern individual is apt to ignore to imbibe what is best in others, but he is quite willing to accept that which debases him in moral evolution. Such being the case, Ashrams should grow in plenty in every nook and corner of the world, particularly in India. Spirituality is the birthright of India, though it is not barred from any other country. Hence, India should take a lead in this direction and illuminate the dark corners of the world where materialism is predominant.

Secondly, religious education should be made compulsory on a common basis without any partiality towards any particular faith. Religious intolerance is partly the cause of so many wars, feuds, dissensions, etc. Education should be imparted free to one and all and it should even be enforced on all alike, boy or girl, adult man or woman. Sastra and Dharma, science and religion, should go hand in hand like twin sisters without any detriment to progress in current worldly affairs.

People should be made to understand that Karma of any nature, provided that it is not against Dharma, does not stand in the way of realising the goal of Moksha and they should be freely allowed to follow their own respective choices so as to shine well in their inclined fields. The age-old traditions, provided they are not a hindrance to graded evolution, should be kept up by all means so as to remind us of the ancient glory of Bharata Varsha. In the name of scientific advancement, old methods of industry and livelihood should not be set at naught; but they should continue to proceed as usual, as rejuvenation of life lies in their survival alone. The Ashrams that manufacture ideal Dheeras in the field of spirituality should undertake to disseminate the knowledge of the Self or Atma-jnana through periodical tours and pilgrimages by their Ashramites.

Periodical spiritual conferences should be held and the methods of Sadhana or Anushthana should be imparted. Such reformatory activities should go on, not only in India but everywhere throughout the world. The lead is willed by the Lord to fall to the lot of India. It is her onerous duty to take it up immediately.

80

How to stop smoking?

Abandon the habit. Take a soothing medicine to counteract nervous excitement. Avoid the company of smokers. Divert the mind to some busy activity. Do not give the mind idle leisure. Study hygienic principles, the laws of good health and ideal life. Impress well upon the mind the ruinous effect of tobacco upon the human system. Observe Ahimsa, Satyam and Brahmacharya. Study spiritual texts and contemplate on their meaning. Practise Asan and Pranayam. Remember God always. All evil traits will vanish.

81

The Gita touches on many subjects which are useful to an aspirant after God-Knowledge, but strangely enough, omits to mention anything about the purpose behind creation. Why did God embark on creation at all?

The Lord's silence, in the Gita, about the purpose of creation, is truly a demonstration of His divine wisdom. This very same problem arises in various minds in various forms. How did Avidya arise in Brahman? When did Karma begin? Why did the Formless assume forms? How could darkness or Maya exist in the Supreme Absolute Light? And so on. There can be no answer to these questions. It involves the understanding of the Ultimate Principle, the Intelligence that is behind and beyond these questions, the Cause of all causes, the Subject of all objects. It cannot be known as an object. And, when the subject (Self or Atman) knows Itself, speech and thought cease. The questioner and question vanish in the quest. The doubt disappears in the doubter. In that Supreme Silence, the problem is inexpressibly solved! The riddle is solved; but speech is baffled—and the question remains unanswerable.

Therefore, the Lord is silent about the transcendental question in the Gita; but, such is the divine wisdom of the Almighty that He gives ways and means of solving the problem.

Don't bother about why creation came into being, but try to know the Creator! Take creation for what it is and try to transcend it. This is wisdom. Trying to probe intellectually into the mystery is only buying psychological distress.

There is no 'Why?' in respect of transcendental matters. 'Why?' is only for worldly things. Reason is finite and frail. God only knows the 'Why?'. Realise the Self. Then you will get the answer. Then you will know the origin and nature of Maya and everything.

82

What do you think of the assassination of Gandhi?

It is the Divine Will that works everywhere. Separation from the body does not mean the death of the person. What one wishes to do, he shall do even after the death of the body. The body is not the real doer of anything. What really does actions is never destroyed. It is not possible to prevent anyone from doing anything by merely killing his body. Gandhiji was a votary of the Second Chapter of the Gita and he knew very well that the Self in him was indestructible.

83

You say, "Atman is our real Self and we are, in reality, universal and absolute". You also say, "The personal relative self involves the idea of individuality, but the Absolute does not....". The question arises—are there two selves? One involving individuality, and the other, without individuality but universal?

There is really one Self which is the Absolute. The relative self is not something different from the Absolute Self, but it is only the Absolute Self experienced through the adjunct or the instrument of the mind. An object has an independent nature of its own, but when it is seen through a distorted coloured glass, it also appears distorted and coloured. It does not however mean from this that the object is both perfect and distorted at the same time; the difference is only in the means of perception and knowledge. This is the case also with the experience of the Absolute Self with the help of the finite mind acting as the instrument of knowledge. The difference is in the medium of perception; the Reality is one.

84

My experience has made me conclude that goodness does not always pay in our dealings with people. Then what is the use of being good and doing good when goodness is not recognized and properly rewarded? Please illumine.

Whether goodness pays you well or not from the material standpoint, do good and be good always. No doubt the worldly-minded generally take advantage of such people as ideal gullibles to carry their wishes through and even to deceive. It matters nothing, for the Lord is always on the side of the good and the righteous who stick to Dharma and who rely on Him. No man is to be considered good without the virtue of piety or God-fearing nature. Goodness and piety go together.

The good man is always the spiritually-inclined, though he is in the world. He is unlike the Vyavaharic Purusha. To be good is to increase the purity and devotion unto the Lord in abundant measure. To do good is to reap good in return. If a good action is done, a sweet fruit in favour of you arises with the result that you enjoy it whether you want it or not. If a bad action is done, the consequent fruit of action liable to be enjoyed willingly or unwillingly will be bitter and against you. Whether goodness is recognized or not, do good and be good throughout life. This alone pays you well to attain Chitta Suddhi and knowledge of the Self. Only those who have no knowledge of the Self, i.e., the worldly-inclined, do not recognize good as a medium of perfection through gradual evolution. Not so is the case with the spiritual-minded, for they know fully well that to do good and to be good help them gain the goal of life, viz., God-realisation.

Remember that the Lord does recognize and reward always the good people and good actions. He actually lives and moves in them. The good man actually feels the Lord's presence in himself and around without a vestige of doubt. It is a mockery for a man to consider himself good without being able to be conscious of God's presence in him, with him and around him. Do not question the benefit of being good and doing good when goodness is not recognized or properly rewarded, for to work alone man has the right and not to the fruits —good or bad—thereof.

85
Will there be world peace if there are no politicians?

World peace would not depend upon the existence or non-existence of politicians, if only people, individually and collectively, understand and live up to the canons of perfect righteousness, wisdom, truth and justice. As long as people do not rise to this level, 'politicians', which is only a name for those who are in charge of the administration, will continue to be actuated by their selfishness and greed and will accordingly ride roughshod over the feelings and sufferings of millions and will go on embarking on wars however destructive they may be in general.

86

I am doing vigorous Tapas and meditation for the last five years. With all that, my troubles and difficulties are multiplying. I have lost my job. I am starving now. What shall I do? Is this the Grace of the Lord? How can I continue my Sadhana when I have nothing to eat?

It is said that the Lord gives food even to the frog that lives between the strata of rocks. Why has He failed in your case alone? This is a great wonder! Has He failed in His duty? This cannot be. He is all-merciful, all benevolent! Is it because He wants to develop in you the constructive qualities—courage, presence of mind, endurance, strong will, fortitude, more mercy and love—and make His instrument more fit for His Divine Lila? Yes, this must be the case.

The struggling and sincere aspirant also gets more troubles and difficulties, because he has to march quickly on the path to reach the portals of the Kingdom of Supreme Peace and Unalloyed Bliss.

Princess Mira renounced the pomp and glory of the palace and walked in the burning sands of Rajputana. She starved on her way to Brindavan. She slept on the ground. She lived on alms. The Pandavas underwent countless sufferings even when Lord Krishna was at their back. Draupadi was placed in a very bad plight even though she had Bhima, Arjuna and Dharmaputra to fight for her. Our sufferings are nothing when compared to the persecutions underwent by the five Pandavas, Sri

Rama and Mira. Look at the sufferings of Raja Harischandra and his wife! He had to serve in the cremation ground and do the work of a Chandala to keep up truthfulness. It is suffering that develops the will. It is suffering alone that moulds a man on the spiritual path. Be not troubled. Feel Lord Siva's grace and mercy at every step. All difficulties will melt away like mist before the sun. Have perfect unswerving faith in His grace.

87

What are the qualifications of a real Guru or a true guide? Is it possible for an ordinary human being to select a real guide? If so, how?

A real Guru is a Srotriya and a Brahmanishtha, one who is learned in the scriptures and established in Brahman. He who is wise, desireless and sinless can be a true teacher and guide. The Guru, by virtue of his wisdom and capacity, draws towards himself the souls fit to be guided by him. When one feels that he is thus spontaneously drawn to a Mahapurusha whom he cannot help loving, admiring and serving, who is an embodiment of unruffled tranquillity, mercy and spiritual experience, such a great one can be taken as the Guru. A Guru is one in whom the disciple can find no defect and who serves as the ideal to be reached by the disciple. In short, the Guru is God in manifested form, and when Divinity is seen in a person, he can be chosen as the Guru. The relation between the Guru and the Sishya is genuine and unbreakable, even as that between God and man is. It is a natural law that when a certain event has to take place in the universe, the conditions necessary for the same are brought about exactly at the proper time. When the disciple is ready to receive the higher Light, he is brought into contact with a suitable Guru by the Supreme Dispensation.

88

How does the mind differ from the Soul?

The mind is a special, limited particularisation of the Soul-consciousness, which is unlimited and never ceases to be all-pervading. The mind is the form of the collective totality of desires, and hence, it is inert and powerless. But it appears to be conscious and powerful as the Inner Self or the Soul is reflected through it. The mind alone is the real person or the individual and it is the real doer of all actions. It is the experiencer of every condition in the universe, both objectively and subjectively. The Soul is the Absolute which is not really affected by any experience of the mind. The mind is mortal, while the Soul is immortal.

89

Our sages and Tapasvins make use of tiger-skins or deer-skins. Does it not amount to sinful violence to kill an animal or get it killed, particularly in the case of those who are out for spiritual advancement? Does it not sound suicidal for a hermit to sit all his life on the skin of a dead animal and aspire for deliverance or Mukti for himself?

The most important point to remember in connection with the use of deer-skin or tiger-skin as Asana or seat is that the animal is never *killed* for obtaining its skin. The deer was always a part of the

ancient Ashrams of Sannyasins and Maharshis; and they should have found the skin of the deer, when it died its natural death, an easily procurable material for the Asan. To those living in dense jungles, therefore, deer-skin and the bark of trees should have been more easily and abundantly available than cloth.

Tiger-skins, too, were procured in a similar way, though much less numerically, and that accounts for the wider use of the deer-skin as Asana. In fact, *Mriga-charma* is prescribed for Asana; and *Mriga* means deer.

From the spiritual point of view, the sages found that doing Sadhana seated on a deer-skin was highly conducive to Siddhi. The power generated in the body through Sadhana was preserved by the skin.

90
Can I practise Pranayam by consulting books?

Yes. You must read the instructions several times and understand the technique thoroughly. If you have doubts, consult some experienced men and then begin the practice. Have regular and systematic practice. If you want quick progress, you must follow my instructions given in the first two chapters of my book "Science of Pranayama". You can gradually increase the period of Kumbhak to two minutes. In the advanced stages of practice, it will be better to have the help of a Guru.

91
Can a married lady practise Pranayam without any harm?

Yogic practices—whatever be their variety—can be resorted to by males and females alike. In the case of those practices that concern the body, like the Hatha or the Kundalini, the woman should observe certain limitations owing to the natural sensitivity of her physical frame. There is absolutely no harm if a woman takes to the practice of Pranayam.

92

Why was Gita taught on the battlefield?

There was some meaning in the Lord's choosing the battlefield for the Gita teaching. Yes. He wanted to point out to us that wisdom should not recline on the arm-chair. If his wisdom did not accompany a man to the field of battle, it was no wisdom at all! Any man could talk philosophy "after dinner"; any man could discourse upon the most intricate points in the Yoga Shastras sitting comfortably near the fireplace. But that is no wisdom at all; it is mere lip-service to the supreme science of Knowledge of the Self. It is hypocrisy. These people generally fail when they face a trial, when their wisdom is put to the acid test of practical demonstration, when they find themselves in a crisis.

Krishna's Panchajanya roars a big 'No'! No, no. That is not wisdom; real wisdom will serve you right on the battlefield, right in a crisis, and will enable you to surmount the obstacle, resist the temptation, arise victoriously from the trial. You will convert the trial into a great opportunity for revealing your genius. For, genius is often made by crisis.

A strong character will not succumb to tests and temptations, however strong and powerful they may be.

On the contrary, a strong character reveals its strength only at the time of such crises. A morally weak man talks philosophy when things are getting on the way he wishes them to; but his philosophy takes leave of him at the sight of a test. Whereas, a morally strong man may give no indication whatsoever of his strength in ordinary times; but when a great trial faces him, he reacts most surprisingly and reveals his character.

That is what Sadhaks should understand from Krishna's choice of the dreadful platform of the battlefield for His discourse. It was, as it were, a fitting prelude to the great Yoga of Equanimity that He was about to preach through Arjuna to the entire humanity.

93

I am practising Sirshasan for a full half an hour. I am not able to cure wet-dreams. What is the fault in my Sadhana? How can I destroy passion?

The practice of Sirshasan for a long time will doubtless help you a lot in destroying your passion. Your thoughts also should be pure. You should not entertain any lustful thought. Have Satsang. Take Sattvic food. Do not look at ladies. Develop Vairagya. Control the Indriyas. All these instructions should be followed if you want sure success. If you happen to entertain lustful thoughts, if you live in the company of lustful persons, and if you do not take Sattvic food, how can you destroy your passion even if you practise Sirshasan for a full three hours?

94

I took Sannyasa recently. Can I have a Parivrajaka life or should I live in seclusion?

For a new student of Sannyasa, strict seclusion for six years with intense Sadhana is essential. It depends upon the condition of your mind. In Parivrajaka life, you cannot have regular and systematic Sadhana. There is distraction everywhere. For some years you should be away from the sensual objects. Strict seclusion will bring immense benefit. Once in a year, for a few days, you can go to a place for change of climate. If you find that you are entering into Tamas, you should combine active service. For a beginner, Nishkama Karma for two or three years will prove good. Then strict seclusion. Occasionally you can have a Parivrajaka life for a few days to test the strength of your mind.

95

I am a married man. I have a great desire to become a Sannyasin. I am disgusted with the family life. I recently lost my child. My wife too is a pious lady. Suppose I take Sannyasa, can I live with her and do spiritual Sadhana?

Now you are not fit for Sannyasa, though you might have a minute trace of Vairagya due to the death of your child. After Sannyasa, you should not live with your wife. You should not remain even in your own place, as Moha will be lurking in a corner of your mind. Old worldly Samskaras will be ever waiting to dupe you. Maya is powerful. You will have to spend all your energy in waging a guerilla war against old Samskaras and temptations. You will have no energy for spiritual practices. Though you may think that you possess a high degree of Vairagya and that your wife also is pious, yet you should be far away from her. You should not even think of her. That is real Sannyasa. What is the meaning of taking Sannyasa and living with your wife and children? How can you destroy Moha, worldly Samskaras and Vasanas?

96

Sometimes, due to cold or some such reason, one of my nostrils gets clogged and the breath does not flow clear and there comes some difficulty in doing Pranayam. What shall I do to make the breath flow freely?

Insert the end of a thread into the nostril. You will begin to sneeze. This will clear the passage. Or lie down for five minutes on the left side if the right nostril is clogged. This also will relieve. Do four rounds of Bhastrika Pranayam. You will be all right.

97

What is the difference between Jivatman and Paramatman?

Jivatman is the individual soul, a reflection of Brahman in Avidya or the mind. Paramatman is the Supreme Soul, Brahman or the Atman. From the empirical viewpoint, the Jivatman is a finite and conditioned being, while the Paramatman is the infinite, eternal, Sat-chit-ananda Brahman. In essence, the Jivatman is identical with Paramatman when Avidya is destroyed.

98

Why has God created young beautiful women? There must be some sense in His creation. We should enjoy them and procreate as many as possible. We should keep up the progeny of the line. If all people become Sannyasins and go to forests, what will become of this world?

These beautiful women and wealth are the instruments of Maya to delude you and entrap you into the nets. If you wish to remain always as a worldly man with low thoughts, debasing desires, you can by all means do so. You are at perfect liberty. You can marry three hundred and fifty wives and procreate as many children. Nobody can check you. But you will soon find that this world cannot give you the satisfaction you want, because all objects are conditioned in time, space and causation. There are death, disease, old age, cares, worries and anxieties, fear, loss, disappointment, failure, abuse, heat, cold, snake-bites, scorpion-stings, earthquakes, accidents, etc. You cannot at all find rest of mind even for a single second. As your mind is filled with passion and impurity, your understanding is clouded and your intellect is perverted now. You are not able to understand the illusory nature of the universe and the everlasting bliss of Atma.

Passion can be effectively checked. There are potent methods. After checking passion, you will enjoy real bliss from within—from Atma.

All men cannot become Sannyasins. They have various ties and attachments. They are passionate and cannot, therefore, leave the world. They are pinned to their wives, children and property. Your proposition is wholly wrong. It is Asambhava, impossible. Have you ever heard in the annals of the world's history that this world had become vacant as all men had become Sannyasins? Then, why do you bring in this absurd proposition? This is an ingenious trick of your mind to support your foolish arguments and Satanic philosophy which has passion and sexual gratification as its important tenets. Do not talk like this in future. This exposes your foolishness and passion-nature. Do not bother yourself about this world. Mind your own business. God is all-powerful. Even if this world is completely evacuated when all people retire to forests, God will immediately create crores of people by mere willing, within the twinkling of an eye. This is not your look-out. Find out methods to eradicate your passion.

99
Through which opening does the soul leave the body?

So long as Prana pulls up and Apana pulls down the life-forces, there is continuity of life. But, the moment either of these becomes weaker, there is an exit of the life-force. If the Apana gives way, then the Jiva will pass out of the body through either the head or the nose or the ear or the mouth. If the Prana gives way, then it will pass out of the body through the anus.

100
What is astral body?

The astral body is the subtle body which is within this physical body like the bladder of a football. It is an exact counterpart of the physical body. It is made up of the five organs of action, the five organs of knowledge, the five Pranas, mind, intellect, Chitta or the subconscious mind, and Ahankar or egoism. Some call it "the double". It is this astral body that comes out of the physical body after death and moves to heaven. Death of this astral body through the knowledge of the Eternal frees one from the cycle of births and deaths.

101

There are 70 lakhs of Sadhus in India and many crores of rupees are spent in vain in feeding these Sadhus. Every Sadhu or a Sannyasin is a parasite on society. Even a Sannyasin should work in the political field. There is no necessity for a life of seclusion or the order of Sannyas or Nivritti Marga. We want workers only.

This is a sad mistake. The Census Report is false. Beggars are included in the list of Sannyasins and Sadhus. Real Sannyasins are rare. They can be counted on the finger-tips. A real Sannyasin is the only mighty potentate of this earth. He never takes anything. He always gives. It was Sannyasins only who did glorious sublime work in the past. It is Sannyasins only who can work wonders in the present and in the future also. Sri Sankara's name can never be obliterated as long as the world lasts. It was Swami Dayananda, it was Swami Vivekananda, it was Swami Rama Tirtha, it was Ramakrishna Paramahamsa, who disseminated the sublime teachings of the scriptures and preserved the Hindu religion. A Sannyasin alone can do any real Lokasangraha, because he has divine knowledge, he is a whole-timed man. One real Sannyasin can change the destiny of the whole world. It was one mighty Sankara who established the doctrine of Kevala Advaita. He still lives in our hearts.

Paramahamsas lived on a few pieces of bread and in exchange moved from door to door and spread the sublime teachings of Vedanta, the Upanishads, the Ramayana and the Bhagavata throughout the length and breadth of India. The world is under a great debt of gratitude to them. Their writings are still a guide to us. Study a few Slokas or verses of the Avadhuta Gita. You will at once be raised to magnanimous heights of divine splendour and glory. You will become a changed man. Depression, weakness, anxieties and tribulations will vanish at once.

Just as there are research scholars or post-graduate students in science, psychology, biology and philosophy, there should be post-graduate Yogins and Sannyasins who will devote their time to study and meditation, to research on Atma. These post-graduate Yogins will give to the world their experiences and realisations in the field of religion. They will train students and send them into the world for preaching.

It is the duty of householders, Zamindars, Rajas and Maharajas to look after the wants of these Sannyasins. In turn, these Sannyasins will take care of their souls. Thus the wheel of the world will revolve smoothly. There will be peace in the land.

Every religion has a band of anchorites who lead the life of seclusion and meditation. There are Bhikshus in Buddhism, Fakirs in Mohammedanism, Sufistic Fakirs in Sufism, Fathers and Reverends in Christianity. The glory of a religion will be lost absolutely if you remove these hermits or Sannyasins or those who lead a life of renunciation and divine contemplation. It is these people who maintain or preserve the religions of the world. It is these people who give solace to the householders when the latter are in trouble and distress. They are the harbingers of divine wisdom and peace. They are the messengers of Atmic knowledge. They are the disseminators of the Adhyatmic science and the Upanishadic revelations. They heal the sick, comfort the forlorn, nurse the bedridden. They bring hope to the hopeless, joy to the depressed, strength to the weak and courage to the timid by imparting the knowledge of the Vedanta and the significance of the *"Tat Tvam Asi"* Mahavakya.

Political Svarajya has been achieved; but can it give real lasting peace and freedom to man? Can this political Svarajya eradicate human sufferings and ignorance in toto? Can this political Svarajya solve the real problems of life? It can give a little more comfort to man. He can have more butter, bread and jam. He will be still miserable and unhappy, because he is still sunk in ignorance; he has no knowledge of the Self. Knowledge of the Self alone can give real lasting happiness and abiding bliss. Atma Svarajya or realisation of Atma or one's own Self alone can make a man really independent and immortal. Atma Svarajya alone can give him real freedom, suzerainty and perfect satisfaction.

Even those who work in the political field should live in the spirit of the Gita and the Upanishads. They should have ethical training, self-control, self-sacrifice, spiritual discipline and understanding of their real nature before they enter the political field. They should practise the three kinds of Tapas—physical, verbal and mental—mentioned in the Gita and the Yama and Niyama of Patanjali Maharshi. They should clearly have a comprehensive understanding of the immortality of the soul, the illusory nature of this world, the unity of Atma or oneness of consciousness, oneness of life. They should understand that the whole world is one family only. Then only they can really serve the country and their own selves.

102

Krishna is not the Lord. He is not an Avatar. He was a passionate cowherd who lustfully played with the Gopis.

What was the age of Lord Krishna at that time? Was He not a boy of seven? Can there be a tinge of passion in Him? Who can understand the secret of Ras Lila and Madhurya Bhav, the culmination of the highest Bhakti, Atmanivedan or total surrender to the Lord? It is only Narada, Suka Deva, Chaitanya, Mira, Hafiz, Ramananda and the Sakhis or Gopis that can understand the secret of Ras Lila. The Sakhis only are qualified for this. Did He not play miracles when he was a boy? Did He not show that He was the Avatara of Lord Hari? Did He not show Virat Darshan to His mother when He was a baby? Did He not kill the Kaliya serpent by standing on its hood? Did He not multiply Himself as countless Krishnas? Who were the Gopis? Were they not God-intoxicated beings who saw Krishna alone everywhere, who saw themselves also as Krishna? The sound of the Murali could throw them into a state of

103

Sri Rama is only an ordinary man. He is not an incarnation of God. He wept bitterly when he lost his wife. His bewailings rent the clouds when Lakshmana fell down on the ground in an unconscious state, being struck by the arrow of Indrajit. Why did Rama, the Supreme Being, forget his real divine nature? He was sunk in the ocean of sorrow at the ordeal of Sita. If Rama always knew his true Self, why did he grieve for the loss of Sita?

The answer to this question is that verily Rama was the Supreme Self. He never moved or did anything. He was never subject to joy or sorrow, birth or death, pleasure or pain.

But, throughout his life, Sri Rama behaved like an ordinary man only. He had to do that, because Ravana had a boon that he could not be killed by Devas, Asuras, Rakshasas, Yakshas, serpents, bears, etc. Ravana, in his pride, had belittled the strength of man and Ravana could be killed only by a man. So Sri Rama had to show that he was an ordinary man only. Otherwise, if Rama had exhibited himself to be a god, according to the boon of Brahma, he would have been disqualified for destroying Ravana.

104

Can a departed spirit take any material form?

Yes. All spirits do not possess the power of materialization. Only advanced spirits that are endowed with psychic power are able to materialize. They take human form, sit in the chair in the seance and shake hands with those who sit in the seance. They talk also. The touch is as tangible and warm as that of a living human body. In a short time, the hand of the spirit melts away. Photographs of the spirits also have been taken.

105

I would like to know very much where my husband's soul is at present. I shall be obliged if you could explain to me what happens to the soul after death and what merits we could do for the peace of the departed soul and whether he could see or hear us, mortals. Is there any truth in what the spiritualists say that we could commune with the dead through a thing called 'medium' and is it really the dead person who answers?

Do not allow yourself to be fascinated by spiritualism, mediumship, crystal gazing, etc. They will lead you astray. Communication with the dead and talking with the dead are all fads which have no connection with real spirituality. The purpose of life is different. The goal is to realise the essential imperishability of your Self. This alone will confer perfect bliss and peace.

The spirit is neither born nor does it die. Like a person passing from one room to another, the soul passes from one plane of existence to another. In the period between death and rebirth, the individual works out a certain portion of his Karmas in subtler spheres. At the appointed time, the soul takes up a new body again.

The best means of ensuring peace for the departed is to do Kirtan, increase your Japa, relieve other people's distress by selfless service and charity, and do earnest prayer.

Do not try to commune with the departed soul of your husband. Communion with the departed soul will stand in the way of its onward march to higher blissful regions and make it earth-bound. Do not try to drag your husband down. It will disturb his peace. The spirit-guide which controls the medium is ignorant and deceitful. It utters falsehood.

106

We should direct all our energies in gaining economic betterment for the masses. If we do not waste time and energy in propagating spiritual ideas, Gita studies and Sankirtan, but devote that energy to the above end, then we shall get economic betterment earlier, after which those who wish can pursue philosophy and religion.

We should develop our material and physical powers and get to the same peak of progress, power and comfort as the Western nations before we can dabble in philosophy and the like.

Two types of workers, social and religious, are necessary in this world. Social workers will work in their own fields of activity. Religious workers will carry on special propaganda and dissemination of spiritual knowledge. A carpenter has his own field of work and an electrician has his own field. You cannot ask a carpenter to do the work of an electrician and the electrician to do the work of a carpenter. Social, economic, political and industrial development and constructive work in those directions are very necessary. These should not be ignored.

But, religion only can save people. Without religion, man is nowhere. Even those who work in the other fields cannot turn out good work without disciplining themselves, without having a spiritual basis, without undergoing a religious training, without practising Ahimsa, Satyam and Brahmacharya. Leaders who are selfish and corrupt spoil the society. They fight for their own superiority and power.

Bread, butter, jam and nice biscuits cannot give you everlasting peace. Comforts are enemies of spiritual life and peace. They pull a man down. After all, man wants very little on this earth. You will think of God only when you are in adversities. What is wanted is spiritual wealth which is inexhaustible.

That work which removes the ignorance of man and gives him happiness can eradicate human sufferings in toto and give him eternal happiness. That work is spiritual propaganda. That work is the dissemination of Bhakti and knowledge of Yoga and Vedanta. It is the crowning glory of human activities. This is the greatest Yajna or Yoga. This is Jnana Yajna, the highest of all Yajnas.

India alone possesses the supreme divine wealth. Even the richest people of the different parts of the world come to the Himalayas to practise Yoga, to seek the guidance of Rishis, seers, Yogis and sages and to acquire this imperishable wealth.

Happiness does not come from wealth. The Western nations are quite restless despite their enormous wealth.

From this we can infer that spiritual life alone can give real, everlasting peace and happiness.

107

How does the Yogi see the subtle rudiments of matter with his Yogic vision?

As you would see the material objects with the help of a material instrument in the form of the eye, the Yogi would see subtler objects through the help of subtler instruments. Except in the plane of intuition, in all other lower planes, there exists a subject-object relationship as far as cognition is concerned. The only thing is: the instrument used in perceiving the object should be of the same material of which the object of perception is made.

For further grasping of the exact vision of the Yogi, you yourself should become one.

108

When everything is predestined and pre-planned by the Lord, why does man endeavour to do and undo things? Should one's repeated failures in respect of a certain work be also taken as the Will of the Lord? Is it a fact that we get what we deserve or is it that we are not really fit for what we actually aspire for? This doubt is eluding a clear-cut answer from my own limited brain. I refer the same to your greater brain to resolve this doubt and I hope you will do so.

It is true that everything is predestined and pre-planned by the Lord; and only in accordance with the holy writ, everything takes place. God has given free will also to the individual to do right or wrong, to discriminate between the Preyo Marga and the Sreyo

Marga. If one is endowed with true wisdom as to the fleeting and painful nature of the worldly enjoyments, one can exert oneself in the right direction to do or undo his Prarabdha, the portion of Karmas ripened for actual experience in this current birth. Without the Lord's special grace, none can make or mar himself. Even for realisation, the Lord's grace is necessary. For obtaining the Lord's grace, intense Purusha Prayatna, otherwise known as Purushartha, which is voiced forth throughout the famous "Yoga Vasishtha" is to be put forth.

Whether it be failure or success in any undertaken work, it is but the effect of the Lord's grace and will alone. Accept everything in the light of Vedantic indifference. Be a silent witness and rejoice over the mystery of the Lord.

Everybody gets what he actually deserves; nothing more, nothing less. The Divine Law is altogether different from man-made law. The Law and Verdict and Judgement of the Lord is final and unquestionable. No bribing business there. His Law is always impartial and uniform and even, with the whole of mankind, why only mankind, with the whole of His own creation.

Aspiration on the mundane side is but an expression of egoism that bursts forth in every moment of man's life through actions, thoughts and speech. Unless it is, as already stated, willed by the Lord, nothing mundane or spiritual is possible of attainment by any human being on earth. God actually helps those that help themselves, provided that the thing aspired for is in strict conformity with the injunctions of the holy writ. From the cradle to the grave, from birth till death, from the moment of awareness to that of eternal rest, the guiding factor of man should be self-effort, self-effort, self-effort and self-effort alone, based on surrender, without minding the results.

109

Though I have attended Satsang all these years and though I have been doing Japa and Dhyan all these years, I have not yet a confirmed belief in God and His Name. There is yet Moha for family, for position, for money and for worldly life. It is strange, Swamiji, I confess.

Maya is powerful, and except in very rare cases where the Samskaras are very strong, taste for a life of contemplation does not manifest itself in man. No doubt, Satsang, Japa and Dhyan help a Sadhak a lot. But the Avarana of Avidya or the veil of ignorance is so thick that these are not sufficient to pierce it. They only create Samskaras which take shape in future births. But, if at the same time you do Vichara, develop Viveka and cultivate Vairagya, then the progress is extremely rapid. Vairagya and Viveka are absolutely necessary. Without these, no amount of Satsang, Japa or Dhyan will produce immediate results. Maya is extremely powerful: she can be annihilated only through Dridha Vairagya, only through intense dispassion.

110

Swamiji, of late I am not able to read my class books. Immediately I take up my class books, I feel that they are not worth studying, since they do not contain the element that would satisfy my hungering soul.

Beloved child! It is too early for you to renounce the world. Besides, you have got your parents. You should serve them nicely. Earn your livelihood by honest means. Work hard. At the same time, adopt the Nimitta Bhav: work as an instrument in His hands. Cultivate this. Carry on your studies also. No doubt, knowledge of this phenomenal world would not confer Moksha on you. Yet, it has got its own uses. Nothing is bad in itself; it is the use to which a particular branch of knowledge is put that matters.

Try to carry on your personal Sadhana also side by side. Practise my *Twenty Important Spiritual Instructions* to the best of your ability. Maintain the spiritual diary. Always keep the goal in view. When the time comes, God Himself will facilitate your renunciation.

111

How are life and meditation intermingled?

There is no man in the world who is not divine by nature. The divinity in man differs only in degree, but not in kind. Even the so-called atheist has got a ray of divinity in him. No man is devoid of the three Gunas — Sattva, Rajas and Tamas — in varying proportions. Whether one is a sceptic or an atheist or a nihilist or some other, that portion of Sattva that abides in man helps him do some virtuous actions, which result in further actions of like nature, either in this birth or in some future births. While he does actions of Rajas and Tamas, he also does Sattvic actions according to the degree of purity and Sattva in him. No man in the world—be he a robber, a thief, a pirate or some other—commits vicious actions alone. Every man commits both virtuous actions and vicious actions in life. That is, he is prone to do mixed actions so long as he is under the grip of Prakriti. When virtuous actions are done, his mind naturally turns towards the divine, however slightly it be. A sense of inner joy he experiences, though he may not be able to express why. Meditation is *essentially* the quality of Sattva. When life is made ennobling, sure is the man to think of God.

In this connection, the point worthy of remembrance is that Sattvic actions themselves are to be considered as worship or meditation. Meditation need not necessarily mean sitting in a lonely corner or sequestered spot and thinking over Rama or Krishna or Jesus or Mohammed or pouring forth verbal or mental prayers. Actions that tend to purify the grossness of the individual are to be collectively treated as meditation. Life is thus meditation coupled with Ajnana to an immeasurable degree in the case of an ordinary individual. If meditation is deliberately taken up on the instructions of a Guru who ought necessarily to be a more evolved soul, man cannot but perform good and selfless actions with Akartritva (non-doership) and Abhoktritva (non-enjoyership) Bhavas to make and feel his life more and more cheerful, more and more enlightening, more and more attractive. In the latter course which is but a *deliberate* step, man evolves more quickly with the speed of lightning, while in the former course man moves forward with the pace of a snail.

Thus, life and meditation are intertwined.

112

Apart from the Guru, do you think that a mediator is necessary in order to enable us to attain Self-realisation?

Yes, yes. That is the Tutelary Deity or Ishta Devata. The mind cannot all at once rise beyond itself. The ego will seldom cut its own throat. Your consciousness will find it a hard task to realise the Cosmic Consciousness. Therefore, the Name and the Form of a Deity are chosen to meditate upon. In due time, this Deity will manifest Itself before you and do the work of annihilating the ego and the mind, enabling you to realise Cosmic Consciousness.

113

What is the need to attain Moksha, Swamiji?

To understand this, you should resort to Satsang and study of scriptures. An intellect that is clouded by all sorts of desires and evil Samskaras will not be able to grasp even the need for Moksha. Such an intellect is Asuric. Read the Gita. Attend Satsang. Listen to the discourses of saints and Sannyasins. Then Viveka will arise in you. You will understand that this world is full of pain and sorrow. The bungalow, the motor-car, the little position and the small salary that you are having now will not then satisfy you. Your aspirations will grow. You will want to liberate yourself.

What great labour goes into the preparation of the microscope lens? After a lot of grinding only you are able to peep into the beyond. Similarly, after a lot of study and Satsang only will your intellect even think of the Beyond.

114

Can a man not lead a good, virtuous life, be charitable, truthful and noble, work for the welfare of the community and die a good man, without aspiring for anything beyond this life?

If you lead a virtuous life and die, you will die as a good man, not as a saint. You will not attain Moksha.

You have hundreds of good men. But, how many saints have you got? Even real aspirants are rare in the world now. Even in your category of "good men", there are grades. How many good men have you got of Gandhiji's type?

What do your good men do? They may be truthful and noble; they may be charitable and pious. But, even they will be selfish at the core. They will hoard wealth and look after only their own wife and children. Will they feel that all children are theirs? When they bring sweetmeats from the bazaar, will they give to other people's children first? No, no. Because they have no knowledge of the truth that the One Self dwells in all beings. Unless this understanding of the Truth dawns on them, unless they meditate upon this Supreme Reality and strive to realise It, how can they develop renunciation and the true spirit of selfless service?

To be a good man is no doubt a better ideal than to be merely a human animal, full of vicious qualities. But it is only a means to an end; it is only a step nearer the goal, not the end or the goal itself. The goal is Self-realisation or Moksha. In order to achieve that, you must be good and do good; and you must do more—you must cultivate discrimination, dispassion and a correct attitude to life; you must meditate, do Japa and Kirtan, study scriptures. Then, by the grace of God, you will attain the goal!

115

What is the technique of concentration on the 18 parts of the body as advised by Sage Yajnavalkya for the purpose of attaining Pratyahara? Please explain fully.

The technique of concentration as given by Sage Yajnavalkya involves a process of withdrawing the mind and Prana gradually and step by step from one part of the body to another, starting from the two big toes of the feet and progressing upward by a series of successive acts of such concentration-cum-withdrawal, through the several occult centres of the body, leading finally to the crown of the head.

By this process, the mind and Prana are totally drawn away from the entire body and finally centered in the top of the head where the practitioner dives into deep meditation.

The 18 parts mentioned by Sage Yajnavalkya are given below:

1. The great toes
2. The ankles
3. The middles of the shanks
4. The parts above the shanks and below the knees
5. The centres of the knees
6. The centres of the thighs
7. The anus
8. The centre of the body, just below the waist
9. The genitals
10. The navel
11. The heart
12. The pit of the throat

13. The root of the palate
14. The root of the nose
15. The eyeballs
16. The centre of the eyebrows
17. The forehead
18. The crown of the head.

It is when the senses are active that the mind becomes outgoing. Thus, concentration is retarded. The senses are made active by the play of Prana. With the withdrawal of Prana, the different parts of the body are rendered quiescent and their activity inhibited. Here, in this technique, the effective withdrawal of Prana is achieved by the withdrawal of the mind. It is not so much by a process of Pranayam as by making use of the interconnection between Prana and the mind that this withdrawal of Prana is effected. When the mind is firmly withdrawn after a short spell of deep concentration upon a particular part, automatically, together with the ingoing mind, the Prana too gets withdrawn. Prana follows the mind.

Thus, stage by stage, the Prana is withdrawn from the big toes upwards right up until it reaches the region of the crown of the head by which time the meditator is, as it were, oblivious of the body. In this state, the meditation proceeds undisturbed and becomes very effective.

This is one of the processes to enter into undisturbed and intense Dhyana. Sit upon your Dhyana Asan. Create the right mood and Bhava by a little chanting of the Pranava Mantra, *Om*. Next, negate the entire phenomenal universe, including this earth. When you reach the state where you are aware only of the body, then commence this process of withdrawal.

Closing your eyes, first direct your entire mind upon the two big toes. Concentrate there. Then gradually draw up the mind from the region of the toes to the next point, viz., the ankles. Now concentrate here. Then withdraw yourself to the third point, i.e, the middle of the shanks. Concentrate here. Next withdraw into the fourth part, and so on. After a few days' progress, depending upon the interest and the earnestness with which you do it, you will be able to go through the entire series of 18 parts and reach the seat, of meditation on the crown of the head within a short time after taking up your seat in the meditation pose.

116

Swamiji, I feel I have not understood the Mahavakyas and their significance properly.

I will explain it to you. Listen attentively.

The first Mahavakya is: "*Prajnanam Brahma.* Consciousness is Brahman". This is Lakshana Vakya. The teacher gives the definition to the student that pure consciousness is Brahman.

Then the teacher says: "*Tat Tvam Asi.* Thou art That. You are the all-pervading pure consciousness". This is known as Upadesa Vakya.

Then the student contemplates on what the teacher expounded, in the form of the idea, "*Aham Brahmasmi.* I am Brahman". This is Anusandhana Vakya.

Finally, the student realises that this Self which is within him is Brahman: "*Ayam Atma Brahma.* This Atma is Brahman". This is Anubhava Vakya.

Have you understood now?

117

I write to inform you that due to excessive practice of Nauli and Uddiyana Bandha and Pranayam, the intestines of my abdomen are aching very severely. It is difficult even to lie on the sides and breathing has become difficult. In spite of all this, I am regularly carrying on my Yogic exercises and Kriyas. Kindly write immediately if there is any cause for alarm. Also suggest some prescription to get rid of this excessive pain on both sides of the lungs.

There is absolutely no cause for alarm owing to the pain that you experience now. Give up Nauli and Uddiyan for three or four days. You can practise even Pranayam without any break, but mind that the Bhastrik type is given up during this period. Have some respite. Do not go to excesses. Bear in mind the saying, *"Ati Sarvatra Varjayet"*. Excess should ever be given up in any matter. Stick to the golden mean.

As regards the type of Pranayam, Sukh Purvak will do for the present, i.e., till such time as you feel better. You will be all right if you give some rest to the abdominal viscera.

When you consider yourself as having attained the normal condition, take to all the Bandhas, Mudras, Kriyas and Bhastrik Pranayam which you may have been practising. Be ever moderate keeping in view that you achieve substantial progress only by modest and sincere efforts and not by immediate, undesirable and indiscreet practices to gain blissful experiences in the twinkling of an eye!

Have open-air walk. Lie on the back in Savasan (corpse pose). Repeat your Ishta Mantra to invoke the blessings of the Lord. Foment the affected parts (ribs) with hot water, with a little turpentine added to it. Sprinkle powder talcum. After fomentation, you can besmear some greasy oil. Relief is sure to ensue.

118

Why are Sadhus and Sannyasins enjoined upon to beg for their food? Don't the sins and evil intentions of the giver of food get mixed up with his charity and thus spoil the mental peace of the Sadhus and Sannyasins by their contaminating influence?

A true Sadhu or a genuine Sannyasin is he who has no attachment to the world even in the slightest degree. Such Sadhus are Brahma-nishtha Purushas (persons in the constant thought of the Divine or Brahman) unmindful of their bare needs even. They should not cook for themselves. Self-cooking induces in any person a desire to prepare this dish or that, to relish this sweet dainty or that. It causes Jihva Chapalya (unsteadiness of the tongue). The aim of all Sadhanas being to control the mind, for which control of the tongue is the best means, self-cooking is prohibited to the Sadhu and the Sannyasin; and in lieu thereof, begging, just to fill up the belly moderately, is allowed. So, begging is no sin for a Sadhu and a Sannyasin.

The fire of Tapas consequent upon Japa, Pranayam, Svadhyaya of the Bhagavata and the like burns all impurities that are likely to affect the God-intoxicated when they take food from ill-evolved and undeveloped souls—be they Brahmins or Pariahs.

119

Why are philosophers called mad? Is there something wrong with the philosophers or the people who call them so?

Compared to the man-of-the-world, a philosopher is a mad person in the sense that the latter cannot take a lively interest in external appearance as the former does. To the philosopher, the external world is only an appearance, but to the man-of-the-world, it is all real and eternal. There is nothing wrong with either of them, since the word 'mad' is used only as a mutual, relative attribute. What the philosopher says, the layman cannot believe; and what the layman experiences, the philosopher cannot.

120

Swamiji, how did Maya arise in Brahman?

This is an Ati-prasna or transcendental question. You will find this question coming up to your mind in various forms: When did Karma begin? When and why was the world created? Why is there evil in the world? Why did the Unmanifest manifest itself? And so on. The same question is asked by Rama in *Yoga Vasishtha* and Vasishtha says: "You are putting the cart before the horse. You will not be benefited by an enquiry into this question at all. Meditate and realise Brahman. You will then know the answer to this question. The problem itself will have dissolved by then". No one can answer this question. When Knowledge dawns, the question itself vanishes. Therefore there is no answer to the question at all.

The Brahma Sutra says: *Lokavat Tu Lila Kaivalyam.* It is only to pacify your doubt. It is really not an answer; for, there can be no answer. Yet, the question will arise in the case of every seeker after Truth. You cannot help it. You will have to use your discrimination, pacify the doubt, and then through intense Sadhana and meditation, realise God. Then the doubt will vanish. A great Yogi and Jnani was worried with this doubt for twelve years. Then he told me: "The worry is over now. It troubled me for twelve years. I could not find an answer. So I have given up that pursuit and have taken to meditation, Japa and Kirtan. Now I find peace and progress". Faith in the Guru, in the Granth Saheb, Kirtan, Japa, meditation and practice of righteousness—these will enable you to progress in the spiritual path and will take you to That where there is no questioning possible.

121

I quite realise that contentment gives peace. But I have a doubt. If I become contented, all my ambitions will die. I will become lethargic and lazy. On account of my various ambitions, I move about hither and thither, I exert and I am energetic. Kindly remove this doubt of mine. I am quite bewildered.

Contentment can never make you idle. It is a Sattvic virtue that propels man towards God. It gives strength of mind and peace. It checks unnecessary and selfish exertions. It opens the inner eye of man and moves his mind towards divine contemplation. It turns his energy in the inner, Sattvic channels. It transmutes the gross energy, viz., greed, that is forcing man towards selfish exertions into spiritual energy, Ojas. That man who is contented is full of Sattva. He is more energetic now. He is inward. He has an inner life in the Atman. He is always peaceful. He turns out more work calmly and with one-pointed mind. All the dissipated rays of the mind are collected now. Do you understand the point now?

It is on the strength of contentment that the Sadhus and Sannyasins, and the Fakirs and Bhikshus move about in the world in a care-free manner by living on Bhiksha. It is contentment that gives strength to an aspirant to walk in the path of Self-realisation and emboldens him to march fearlessly in the rugged and thorny path of spirituality.

122

In all matters with which it is connected, science gives us a precise account of how a particular thing is constructed and how it grows. We are also given the successive signs that mark the growth. Are there, in the practice of Yoga, any definite indication to measure the aspirant's progress—for instance, some experiences that he would have after, say, three months of practice, others which he would come upon after a year, and so on?

Various Yogas give various experiences. The practice of Pranayam and Hatha Yogic Kriyas, for instance, would give a graded series of psychic experiences. Seeing all kinds of ethereal lights and hearing certain Anahata sounds belong to this category. Here, the sages who have propounded these Yogas have given very definite stages of spiritual experience. As the

Kundalini passes from Chakra to Chakra, the Yogi has certain definite, verifiable experiences. That is because each Chakra governs a particular Tattva, and its mastery, therefore, gives specific experiences.

Similarly, in Tantrik Sadhana also, they have been able to give a definite chart of spiritual experiences. Each Sadhana has its own particular Siddhi; and therefore, the experiences of all Sadhaks following a particular Sadhana are invariably the same.

But, these are all lower experiences of an inferior type. They are psychic experiences which need not necessarily denote the aspirant's spiritual progress. Even the Bhakta's experiences of horripilation, shedding of tears, etc., though they are not so perfectly graded as those of the Hatha Yoga practitioner, do not necessarily indicate spiritual progress.

When you enter the domain of the Spirit, you come into the sphere of the Infinite. Infinite are the Yogas and infinite are the experiences too. Each man's Yoga is his own. For, he has brought his own Samskaras and Vasanas and he strives in his own way to reach the goal. These two, interacting on each other, give him his various experiences. For instance, as he approaches the transcendental, infinite, immortal Self, the aspirant would enjoy great inner peace and indescribable happiness. He is not easily affected by what goes on around him. Not only this, he is able to radiate peace and happiness to all those who come into contact with him. He becomes *good* and radiates goodness. This is the most important sign of spiritual progress. God is perfect goodness. The aspirant who progresses towards the realisation of God, therefore, grows in goodness. His evil qualities slowly vanish and are replaced by sublime virtues. If this most essential element is not there, then all other visions and sounds are practically useless. By his mere presence the advanced Yogi is able to inspire people to lead a good life, free from hatred and malice. His heart is filled with cosmic love, and therefore, he serves all spontaneously and selflessly. These are all real signs of spiritual progress.

But, beyond all these, is the ultimate experience. That is indescribable. Peace and happiness, undisturbed tranquillity of mind—these are all great signs of progress, but they do not constitute the goal. The goal is to become God. You must become one with God. This is achieved through ceaseless practice of meditation after establishing oneself in virtue and goodness. That supreme experience, when the Yogi feels he is one with God, no words can describe.

123

How was it possible for Sri Sankaracharya to have devotion to Sakara Brahman when he was an Advaitin and his philosophical treatises prove that he believed in the nameless and formless One?

It is because Jnana and Bhakti are essentially the same! Look at the various Stotras that he has composed. They indicate clearly that he had developed devotion to a very high degree. Atmanivedan or self-surrender leads to Jnana; and Jnana is synonymous with Para Bhakti.

People nowadays condemn Bhakti and think that it is inferior to Jnana Yoga. They have no understanding of Bhakti. They think that they can jump at once to Jnana Yoga Sadhana. They have really no faith in God. They just acquire some intellectual conception of God. This does not serve them. Jnana Yoga without the necessary preparation is of no use.

124

Swamiji! I find a few places like Nagore, Shirdi, Tiruvannamalai and Rishikesh ever full of Shanti and a kind of spiritual bliss. May it be, Swamiji, that these places which have had the impress of the saint's personality, his Tapasya and Siddhi, on the very atmosphere, retain that sanctity for a long time?

Yes, yes. And not only that. The saint himself may live in those places. The liberated sage has the option to merge in Brahman or to live in a subtle form and carry on the work of Lokasangraha, guiding aspirants, awakening in people a religious fervour and so on. This motive is manifested in some Jivanmuktas in accordance with God's supreme will. Therefore, the place in which the saint practised Tapas and attained Siddhi, which might again be chosen by the invisible spirit of the saint as its permanent abode, becomes the abode of the saint's divine qualities—peace, bliss and wisdom.

125

The senses are generally turned outside. It is said that if they are turned inside, one will be able to attain Mukti. What is meant by turning them inside?

Now, think of Lord Rama and repeat *Ram, Ram.* When you mentally repeat *Ram,* keep a picture of Ram. The senses will be withdrawn.

Now the eyes run towards objects and the ears run to various sounds. When you repeat *Ram, Ram* loudly, the ears hear only *Ram, Ram;* and they will not run. The inner eye will see only Ram's picture. The mind will be concentrated on God. It will not run towards objects. So, gaze within, introspect. You can do Pranayam also. Stop the breath. It is Prana that gives strength to the senses. You withdraw the Prana and try to centralise it so that the senses have no vigour to run outside. By gradual practice, the senses will be absorbed in the mind. The mind will be concentrated and will be absorbed in the Self. That is superconscious state, Samadhi. Daily practise.

126

Is it possible to become absolutely desireless? The Western psychologists say that it is impossible to give up all desires.

Western psychologists are babies. In the *Yoga Vasishtha* and in Patanjali's *Yoga Sutras,* it is mentioned that absolute desirelessness is Moksha. A Jivanmukta has no desires. Desire is imperfection. A Jivanmukta is a perfected soul. How can there be desires in him? How can perfection and imperfection go together? So, it is quite possible to be free from all desires.

127

Psychologists do not accept that there is a superconscious state. They accept only the conscious and the subconscious states.

An owl says, "There is no light". Is there no light? Similarly, the 'owl' professor says that there is no superconsciousness. Because an owl professor says that there is no superconsciousness, does superconsciousness cease to be? Study *Yoga Vasishtha* which affirms the existence of superconsciousness. He who denies superconsciousness is like the owl that denies light simply because it cannot see light.

128

I am not able to practise meditation for more than ten minutes. After that my mind begins to wander on sensual objects.

When you develop Ruchi or taste for Dhyana and Japa, you will be able to sit longer for Japa and meditation. Increase Japa and meditation. Before going to bed, also in the morning at 4 o'clock, and before taking meal at noon, you should do Japa and meditation. Just as you take tea three or four times a day, so also, you should do Japa three or four times a day. Do not worry if the mind wanders. By gradual practice, it will come under your control. Do Kirtan when the mind wanders much. Do Nama-smaran while walking and working also—*Sri Ram, Sri Ram.*

If you are not able to sit in Padmasan for long, you can sit on a sofa and do Japa and meditation. It is not necessary that you should sit in Padmasan.

Give up onions and garlic completely. Give it up entirely. Do not prepare it at all at home. If you try to reduce it, one day you will take a little, another day you will be tempted to take a good quantity! A cigarette addict who wants to reduce cigarettes, takes a very few cigarettes on some days, but on some other days he smokes heavily, with a vengeance as it were, and more than compensates for the quantity foregone by him previously. Therefore, give up onions completely.

If you give nice cotton seeds and oil-cakes to your cow, it will cease to graze in your neighbour's fields, it will give up its wandering habit in search of grass and herbs. Now your mind is running after *Rasagulla* and *Peda* which it has tasted. But if you give the mind the bliss of Japa and meditation, it will no more run after worldly objects. When you develop Ruchi for Japa and meditation, the mind will give up its wandering habit.

129

I am in something of a dilemma due to the fact that I do not know what my aim in life is to be. I have been told that if I know this, I will find it easier to meditate. Could you tell me how to discover the answer to this?

The aim of life is God-realisation. To become one with Jesus is the goal of life. To transmute the brutal instincts and to become divine is the goal of life. If you control anger, eradicate selfishness and develop tolerance, compassion, selflessness, generosity, courage, forgiveness, you will become divine. Is selfishness good? No. So become selfless. Is greediness good? Is anger good? Is lust good? Is vanity good? These form the lower nature of man. So remove these and become selfless, generous, patient, tolerant, pure and humble. This is the goal.

130

Will not one be violating one's Dharma by embracing Sannyas and by not discharging his duties to his parents and dependants? Are one's relatives really dependent on him?

The notion that others depend on you is due to sheer delusion. God alone takes care of everyone. Being deluded, you think that you are supporting your kith and kin and undergo endless troubles, miseries and vexations. Even if you turn an anchorite, God will arrange everything and maintain your family. And no sin will accrue to you, provided you have intense Vairagya. Swami Ram Tirth had burning Vairagya; so he resigned his job, and leaving behind his wife and two young sons, took to Sannyas. Similarly, Lord Buddha renounced his kingdom and turned a recluse.

131

Can a person really help others in this world, or is it that such an idea is due to a delusion in the mind? Is it not true that a man can rise or fall only as a result of his own Karma and that the Karmas of others can have no effect on him? Are not the circumstances that a person meets with earned by his own actions? Can a person take initiative and change the circumstances of himself as well as of others?

Surely one can take the initiative. He can do good to himself and to others. He can determine the circumstances and environments. Just see how much one can do for others, how much one can really assist them in the relative plane. One can impart knowledge to the illiterate and the ignorant, extend monetary help to the poor and the needy.

One can educate the orphans and contribute to the institutions that take care of the children. Indeed, one can spend not only his entire earnings, but something more! Why should there be any doubt in regard to one's being really helpful to others? Take the example of Gandhiji. Did he not do immense service and good to the nation and to the world at large?

132

What is the easiest method of developing devotion?

The easiest method of developing devotion is to hear again and again the Lord's Lilas. Each time you hear the Lord's Lilas and glories, an image of the Lord is formed in your mind. And when you go on hearing the glories of the Lord, in due course, the Lord's image in your mind gets strong and bright, even as the piece of wax which a goldsmith uses for collecting the gold particles which fall on the ground while cutting gold pieces, accumulates gold in it every day, and after some days, itself begins to shine like a piece of gold, when the maximum number of gold particles have stuck to it. And when the form of the Lord is bright and firm in the mind, the devotee has ceaseless remembrance of Him and surging devotion for Him.

133

Can we practise Kundalini Yoga by ourselves without the direct guidance of a Guru?

No, that will lead to all kinds of complications. You should have an expert Guru by your side to practise Kundalini Yoga.

But why do you worry so much over the awakening of the Kundalini through Hatha Yoga methods? Any

Sadhana, properly done, will awaken the Kundalini. Kundalini can be awakened through Bhakti, through the grace of the Guru, through the constant practice of Nishkama Karma Yoga, through Vedantic Vichar and through meditation. Through total self-surrender to the Lord and by becoming completely desireless, you can get all psychic powers. Nama-smaran, combined with selfless service, is the best Yoga for this age. You will get the Lord's grace, and with His grace, His divine Sakti will flow into you. What can you not achieve through that ? These psychic powers are all hindrances and obstacles on the spiritual path. We should not run after them. If we go on serving humanity, even if we have unconsciously acquired psychic powers through the practice of Bhakti or Karma Yoga, we will be unconsciously utilizing them for the good of humanity, without being tainted by them. That is the best method.

134

Swamiji Maharaj! What is your idea about Nirguna Brahman? Does it mean only Shunya? In that case, it does not very much appeal to us. Who would like to meditate on nothingness?

Nirguna is not nothingness. It is the fullness of everything that is good. Nirguna is plenitude. In it you find all auspiciousness, all goodness, all beauty, all joy, all health, all sweetness, all purity, all peace, everything developed to perfection. From a distance this fullness becomes inconceivable and so the sages called it Nirguna. Once they reach there, they get merged in that inexpressible experience. It is not nothingness, but it is everythingness, and beyond this too, for it is inexpressible. Only know that all that exists in Maya or false perception, viz., evil, ugliness, misery, change, birth, decay, death, etc., are not in It. For, It is beyond Maya. In Nirguna Brahman, there are no Gunas of Maya, viz., blue colour, etc. That is what is meant by Nirguna.

135

Swamiji, I have often come across this word 'Kala' in the Indian scriptures. What exactly is meant by it?

It is the Great Time personified. It is the destroyer of name and form. In the Hindu pantheon, there are various gods and goddesses who are members of the divine hierarchy. Just as we have our government here composed of various ministers and officers, the celestials who rule the world, too, have their own deities who control the various aspects of creation, preservation and destruction of this world. Some are in charge of the various elements like air, fire and water; some are in charge of birth, death, preservation of life and disease. Kala or Yama or Dharmaraja is the Lord of Death. The entire universe is under his control in a way; for, when the time comes, he brings about the end of the earthly sojourn of all beings. It is only the man of Self-realisation who transcends this Kala and realises his own Self. All Sadhana is meant to help us transcend this Kala, to conquer death, to go beyond time.

136

Please explain to me what is meant by Cosmic Consciousness.

It is a state of consciousness in which you are aware that God is all that there is, and what is more, that He is the link that connects all individuals. God is the Consciousness that illumines the entire creation. Realisation of this Consciousness or God liberates one from bondage to passing phenomena, from the illusion of names and forms. This is the state of God-realisation or Self-realisation.

After God-realisation, the individual is completely merged in the Cosmic Consciousness or God. It is like the rivers entering into the ocean; they lose their identity and you can no more distinguish the waters of the Ganges from the waters of the Godavari. The appearance of the world vanishes in the Reality of God, just as when the lamp is brought, the snake which appeared to be vanishes in the rope that exists.

137

How to free ourselves from Karma, Swamiji?

Feel, as you do your daily duties, that you are only a witness of all that goes on around you, of even your own actions. This is called Sakshi Bhav. You should inwardly realise that you are different from the active principle in you. This is the method of Vedanta.

There is the other—easier, but equally potent—method of Nimitta Bhav. Feel that the Lord alone is the real doer of all actions and that you are an instrument in His hands. Your actions will be transformed into worship of the Lord, and you will not be bound to them. Work without expectation of any reward and without egoism. Root out the idea of agency; feel, "I am not the doer". You will be freed from the shackles of Karma. You will not accumulate new Karma. Allow your Prarabdha Karma to work out; and you will attain liberation.

138

In our quest after Truth, Swamiji, I can understand that great Saviours like Lord Jesus can help us. But it is not always that such souls are present amidst us. What are we to do, Swamiji?

Saints are always present in the world. Rogues are also always present. Saviours and dacoits are ever present in the world; for, it is a world of dualities. Good and evil are ever present here. Absolute good can be found only in God. You should get the guidance of saints; only they can teach you the Brahma Vidya. Books will certainly help you; they will put you in tune with the great ones. When you read the Bible, you are in tune with Lord Jesus. When you read the Gita, you are in tune with Lord Krishna. This also will help you. But, just as you cannot learn cooking from books, you cannot also learn Yoga from books alone. But, you should not indefinitely wait for a teacher to turn up; when the aspiration arises in your heart, you should at once start the practice with the help of some scriptural text your mind likes the most, e.g., the Bible.

139

Are the senses meant to be starved and destroyed? The ascetic ideal says so.

The Greek ideal, however, is moderate enjoyment of life. Most of the Western thinkers of the rationalistic type accept this.

Modern psychologists assert that by denying or refusing the needs of the body such as food and sex and suppressing emotions like attachment and love, people generally create mental problems for themselves. Is there any substance in this?

No; the senses have *not* been given only to be starved or killed. Neither are they given for being indulged in and fattened. In truth, the senses are not given for any earthly purpose whatsoever. That is the highest view that the sages uphold for spiritual aspirants. The senses are given for being utilized consciously and deliberately for the attainment of something altogether above and beyond the farthest reach of the senses. To understand the right import and significance of self-restraint, one must take a more comprehensive view of the question.

In the human being, these senses are given together with the superior, directive faculty of intelligence with its aspects such as discrimination, selection, etc. The senses are to operate under its wise supervision. The aim is not the ultimate denial of the senses, but the achievement through restraint, of a pleasure a millionfold greater than that achieved through gratification. When one realises this fact, he will understand, how, with the Yogic aspirant, this self-restraint is not a matter of bitterness or reluctant, unwilling repression at all. Understood in its correct light, it is a joyous, voluntary discipline undertaken for the acquisition of an infinitely greater and more blissful experience. Does the angler ever grudge the loss of the worm cast for catching a big fish?

Moreover, the rationale of asceticism is not rightly understood by most people. The ideal of asceticism and penance is not based upon repression. Conservation and sublimation are the principles underlying asceticism rightly practised. The true ascetic withholds, diverts, canalizes and finally transmutes his natural propensities. The untoward repercussions of forced repression such as complex, neurosis, etc., have no place here. No doubt, modern psychologists are correct in their view about repression, but one must know that it does not apply to religious asceticism, wherein the process is sublimation and not just repression; and it must always be remembered that asceticism is a part of Yoga which provides such a marvellous system of mental training and culture that most effectively counteracts and wards off any possibility of neurotic complexes or obsessions.

It is, however, true that asceticism is very much misunderstood by the majority of persons, and unfortunately by the ascetics themselves, as a result of which we hardly come across a real ascetic in the aspirant world.

Yoga recommends a proper utilization of the tremendous faculties of undissipated senses for higher purposes of inner culture, social welfare, inventions, scientific progress, and finally, intuition. The senses are to be sublimated through restraint applied through reason and intelligent judgement. Their unlimited potentialities are to be harnessed for the greater good and not allowed to be most shamelessly dissipated for a momentary pleasure, unintelligent and animalistic. Viewed from this angle, the aspirant is asked not to starve and destroy the senses, but really to strengthen them and utilize them for his good. Dissipation, on the contrary, actually causes destruction of the senses.

The Greek ideal was enunciated as a general philosophy of life for the average humanity. Asceticism, as understood by the sages, is a distinctive discipline specially incumbent upon that class which would walk the spiritual way, the aspirant class dedicated to the goal of Self-realisation. This class is vividly aware that the conception of "moderate enjoyment of life" is a conception alone and is well-nigh impossible to put into actual practice. For, the very nature of enjoyment is such that it tends to progressively increase in force each time the senses are indulged in. The habit gets man in its grip and drags him down. This has been the uniform experience of the sages. Therefore, at one stage or the other, a rigid religious self-control and denial becomes imperative in the march to spiritual progress.

The rank materialist may not care for it, but the seeker does. The seeker is marked out for a special achievement. You know how an ultra-modern acrobat, a ballet dancer or an expert boxer willingly imposes a rigid regimen upon himself to keep perfectly trim and healthy for his professional success. Mark the denials and restrictions during the training period of any serious candidate trying for a championship in athletics! His keen zest and enthusiasm serve to keep his mind in a high mood of inspiration and anticipation. What, then, should be the interest and aspiration in true asceticism undertaken as a part of the training for an infinitely greater achievement in the spiritual path?

140

How to remove indigestion?

Eat when you are hungry. Do not eat anything between meals. Eat slowly in a calm mood. Chew properly. Eat moderately. Avoid many combinations of food. Drink a glass of water one hour before or after food, never with a meal. Fast on Ekadasi. Eat nothing before 9 a.m. or after 7 p.m. Take care of your teeth. Just before or after a meal, avoid all exertion, mental or physical. Relax at least for half an hour. A long brisk walk is beneficial. Paschimottanasan, Halasan, Bhujangasan, Salabhasan, Dhanurasan, Mayurasan—these Yogasans will remove indigestion. Depression of mind, cares, worries and anxieties also affect the stomach. Be cheerful. Be regular in your Japa.

141

What is the best method to check the advance of lust?

Lust is but a natural tendency of the mind. The best method to check the impulse is the way of intense and deep Vairagya by a study of religious books, by constant Satsang with Mahatmas (noble souls), by self-enquiry or "Who am I?" enquiry, by close observance of the ways of the world, and by an understanding of the diseases and the spiritual degradation that result from over-indulgence. Remember the saying of the Lord in the Gita:

Trividham Narakasyedam Dvaram Nasanamatmanah
Kamah Krodhastatha Lobhas Tasmat Etat Trayam Tyajet

(Ch. XVI-21)

Practise the chief Asans and Pranayam as detailed in my books "Yoga Asanas" and "Science of Pranayama". Do intense Japa to the point of self-forgetfulness. Treat womankind as the manifestation of the Devi, the adorable Mother Divine. Maintain Matru Bhav in your dealings with the other sex. Give up looking at the face of a woman, but look at her feet to avoid room for evil thoughts to crop up or indiscriminate deeds to arise. Take cold water bath always. Control the tongue. To give leniency to the tongue means to allow free access to lust to trouble the being. Always engage yourself in pure and noble thoughts. Realise the glory of Brahmacharya by studying the lives of Hanuman, Ramdas, etc. Check yourself as per the details given in my book, "How to Get Vairagya". Reduce wants and desires. In proportion to the reduction of the egoistic self, all negative tendencies will disappear.

142

What view do you hold about cow-slaughter? Do you believe that its practice is the main cause of the downfall of our nation?

Scriptures, and the personages and episodes in the scriptures, are as true as God Himself. The former definitely and unambiguously say and propound that all the thirty crores of Devatas as envisaged in Hinduism have their abode in the frame of the cow, as in the Basil plant (Tulasi). The cow is boldly proclaimed in the scriptures as one of the objects of Dana (offering) for the uplift of the soul when the Prana departs from the body of a human being. The cow is really worthy of our adoration. Pancha Gavya (the milk, curd, Ghee, urine and dung of a cow) are ordained to be taken in for Prayaschitta at the commencement of certain Vratas like Rishi Panchami. Any number of instances can be cited regarding the holiness of a cow. Go-puja (cow worship) is as much fruitful as Sannyasi (Sadhu) Puja. It is equal to, if not more than, Sakala Devata Puja (worship of all deities). Such being the case, cow-slaughter (Go-Vadha) is *condemnable* without hesitation.

143

It is mentioned in our Puranas that in days of yore Akashvani was frequently heard by our ancestors who were forewarned by it of coming events. Is it credible? Or, was it only the voice of their own inner intuition?

There is some order in the four Yugas. The consciousness of man grows grosser and grosser as time rolls by. In the previous Yugas, man's consciousness was subtler than it is in this Yuga.

In the Satya Yuga, Bhagavan used to move amidst mankind. Human consciousness was not far removed from divine consciousness. In the Treta Yuga, man's consciousness grew grosser. Though God was not constantly moving amidst human beings, there were frequent Avataras of the Lord. In the Dvapara Yuga, man's consciousness grew grosser still; and only the immortal Brahma-Rishis like Narada, Visvamitra, etc., used to move amongst men, and also, Akashvanis used to warn people of coming events.

Now we feel that Akashvani is a very rare and miraculous thing; in the previous Yugas it was not so. Devas themselves used to move amongst men. And

Akashvani used to forewarn the people regularly. Just as we have our Government, the celestials also have their own Government. Whenever they wished to communicate with mankind, they used to do so through Akashvani.

Nowadays the deity communicates with the people mainly through dreams and visions. That is practically the only form of communication with human beings that Devas have retained in this Yuga.

144

There is a general complaint that Swamiji Maharaj, who is supposed to be above all caste, creed, religion and sex, is always surrounded by lady visitors, mostly. Pray, kindly answer this question.

I do not prevent men from sitting around me. In fact, in the office, there are quite a number of them always surrounding me. They sit on the bench provided for visitors; and the ladies, naturally in keeping with Indian tradition, sit on the ground, around my table. While walking about, the European custom prevails; and the men, of their own accord, let the ladies first. Therefore, the ladies seem to crowd round me and the men walk a few paces behind.

But, when all is said and done, no one can deny that women have more devotion than men who have been endowed with more of intellect. It is the ladies' devotion that makes them sit near my table in the office; and it is the men's intellect that makes them question the propriety thereof! When the intellectual man cultivates devotion too, the result is an understanding heart and breadth of vision that lead him soon to Self-realisation.

I am as much interested in the spiritual welfare of women as in that of men; perhaps I take a little more interest in guiding women on the path of Sadhana. There are three reasons for this. Firstly, you know the wise saying: "The hand that rocks the cradle rules the world". Woman is the maker of man; if she is spiritual, then there is no doubt that the whole of mankind would be pious and peaceful. Secondly, while men all over the world are busy running after the shadow, trying to acquire wealth and the useless objects of this world, it is the women who preserve Dharma as best as they can. They need all the spiritual strength and encouragement that we can provide them. Thirdly, as man's "better half", I know that if woman is spiritually inclined, she will not leave her man behind, but will take him along with her on the spiritual path. She is man's 'Sahadharmini', and even if in the busy work-a-day world man forgets his role for a while, woman will not; and she will be patiently working for his welfare and will convert him to the life divine.

145

Swamiji, while you always associate saintliness with humility, why are you so fond of being photographed?

The force behind the system of visual education which psychologists today acclaim as infinitely superior to text-book education will be apparent if you reflect over a very common phenomenon. Leave on your table in the study a few good books, a few pictorials and a few photographs. Let your children, your friends, come into the study. What do they pick up first? The books? No. The photographs first, and then, the pictorials.

It is not entirely without reason that the old women in South India prevented their grandchildren from being photographed, saying, "Your lustre will be taken away by the photograph". It is true that your lustre is transferred to the photograph. To your friends and relatives, to your near and dear ones, your photograph is alive, aglow with your lustre. Therefore, to a devotee, a picture of the Lord, and to a disciple, a picture of the Guru, is a Living Presence. It is necessary for meditations.

Why are there so many photographs, you may ask. Different people want different photographs, in different poses, with different backgrounds. I have to satisfy all of them. A photograph of mine taken twenty years ago may look more youthful and may be better technically than the photograph taken today; but the aspirant who has seen me for the first time today insists that he should have a photograph of me as I am today and does not accept another taken twenty years ago, however nice it may be. And then, people want to be photographed with me; these photographs act as mementos of their visits and inspire the visitors.

Refusing to be photographed is subtle egoism. It is timidity or fear of criticism in the garb of humility. If you have right discrimination, you will at once understand.

146

Why should a great saint like you, who has renounced everything, put on an overcoat in winter?

A saint or a Sannyasin will not sleep on thorns, eat mud and stones, walk on his head and break through walls. His body, too, is subject to hunger and thirst, heat and cold, etc., and an overcoat is only a vertical blanket in bits and stitched in a convenient way to cover the body against cold without hampering the movement of the limbs for service. A blanket is a horizontal piece. I do not attach more importance or value to the coat.

After all, why should you look at the outer garb? Try to perceive the inner man, his thoughts, his ideas and his virtues. Not the external details. Only a real saint can understand another saint.

It is not a body besmeared with ashes, or a flowing beard or matted locks that determine a saint. Why should you attach much importance to this overcoat of mine? To indulge in dress by way of luxury is certainly not justified. But, for bare necessities, the body must be provided with proper dress and food.

147

Why are you fond of publicity? You talk of selfless service so much; and yet, we find you working for name and fame!

Firstly, I am not *working* for name and fame. When a person does selfless service, fame comes to him, though he does not want it. You found it so in the case of Mahatma Gandhiji's life also. Only selfless persons know how to utilize even that fame for doing more selfless service to a greater number of persons.

Secondly, it is through publicity that I come into contact with more and more seekers after truth. It is the publicity that enables more and more people to offer me opportunities to serve them. When people glorify me, they glorify only Sannyasa, they glorify a divine life of Sadhana; and if by bringing this to the notice of others, they too can be inspired to lead the divine life, practise Sadhana for attaining Self-realisation, I do not neglect it. As you know, lives of great men remind you that you can make your life sublime.

Thirdly, the man who runs after name and fame would not do menial service, would not mix freely with everybody, would not cut jokes and make people laugh in his presence; he would keep himself "far above" the common run of mankind, compel the awe and reverence of the people, and by artificially dwelling on high philosophical themes alone during his conversations, would endeavour to impress on those who meet him that he is far above all of them. I like to mix with all and to make everybody feel that I am one with all. I take intense delight in doing every kind of service to everybody. I am full of educative humour; even a young boy can cut jokes with me.

Please come here and spend some time in the Ashram. You will change your opinion.

148

Can asceticism lead to enlightenment?

Asceticism is really the austere life of sense-control and mental concentration lived for the purpose of devotional practices or spiritual meditations. True asceticism necessarily includes a strict observance of the moral and ethical disciplines, on the basis of which the higher practices are undertaken. Asceticism is a means to enlightenment in as much as it prepares the ground for meditation which leads to wisdom and realisation. Sometimes, asceticism is taken in its narrower sense of bodily mortification alone. But this is a grave error and this alone cannot lead to enlightenment without the calming of the passions and discipline of the mind.

149
Life and death—which is more dreadful?

Life and death are both processes of gaining more and more fresh experiences in the progress of evolution tending towards the fruition of the wishes of the experiencer. Life is a scene where the individual puts on the dress or the form of a certain amount of desires which can be fulfilled in the special environment afforded by it; and death is the time when the individual goes behind the screen and puts on a new dress to appear in another scene of life in order to fulfil another quality of desires which cannot find the required atmosphere for fruition in the present life, but demand a fresh suitable environment. Hence, when properly understood, neither of them is dreadful. Both are necessary processes of breaking the barriers and tearing the veils in the path to Perfection. To the ignorant man, however, both are dreadful experiences. He imagines death to be more dreadful.

150
What is this earth?

Different definitions can be given from different standpoints. The earth is one of the fields for experiencing the fruits of good, bad and mixed actions, and for performing fresh actions. It is a Bhoga-bhumi as well as a Karma-bhumi. It is a bundle of atoms, a form of energy, a materialization of thought, an expression of the effects of the Karmas of the individuals of whom it is composed and to whom it is related. Scientifically, the earth is only one of the planets which go to make the universe.

151

In an Ashram where you have gathered together young spiritual aspirants, promising to guide them in their rapid march to the Goal of life, viz., Self-realisation, why do you encourage dance, drama and music?

The question betrays an ignorance of the fundamental principles of music and dance. They are divine. I should request you to remember that Lord Krishna with His inseparable flute and Mother Sarasvati with Her Veena remind you that music is divine. Lord Nataraja reminds you that dance had its origin in Him. The wickedness of man would misuse anything. Because pickpockets are found in abundance in a temple on a festival day, should we deny ourselves the blessings of His Darshan?

It is a pity that these two divine arts—music and dance—have been brought down to the level of sensuous entertainment. It is the sacred duty of every lover of God and of the fine arts to raise them to their original standards of purity and divinity.

Music is Nada Yoga. It at once enables you to attain union with Nada Brahman, the sacred Pranava. Nritya or dance enables you to enter into Bhava Samadhi.

Drama is a very powerful instrument for the dissemination of spiritual knowledge. What you cannot teach through hundreds of books and hours of lecture, you can bring home to the audience easily and effectively through a single play. Drama is an art-form that touches the heart.

The very fact that the worldly man has taken such an interest in these three and misused them to fulfil his nefarious purposes, shows what a tremendous power they have over the heart and soul of man. What a blessing they will be if they are used for spiritual ends!

152

Why haven't you engaged yourself in the active field of service to humanity, Swamiji, just as Gandhiji had done? Unlike him, you have secluded yourself on the banks of the Ganges without entering the political field at all.

God has endowed each man with certain talents and marked out the field of service for him. Wisdom lies in finding out those talents and utilizing them in selfless service to humanity, in accordance with His will. Gandhiji's was a political field of service. Mine is the field of renunciation, Sannyas and Nivritti. For us to exchange places would be like a cobbler and a tailor exchanging places!

But, do not allow the mind to form the impression that only that man who indulges in politics serves the Lord's children....

153

Why is suicide considered a sin?

Pleasure and pain in life are respectively the rewards of the good and the bad actions of an individual. If a man suffers, it is a reminder to him to ennoble his life and make his future happy through the performance of good deeds, self-discipline and right effort.

When a person, convicted to a term of imprisonment by the court of law for having committed an offence, escapes from the prison, the law demands that he should be rearrested and given added punishment, because he had not only committed an offence but tried to avoid the punishment therefor. So is the case with trying to escape from one's suffering by inflicting death on oneself, rather than attempting through self-effort to improve one's future or accepting philosophically what is beyond all help.

One has, besides, no right to take a life, even though it may be his own, since it is a crime not only in the eyes of God but also in the eyes of social law. The person who commits suicide will suffer more in a spirit-body for a period of time, and then take a lower form of birth, to work out his Karma. So, one will not be benefited in any way by committing suicide.

154

The Atman is different from the body and is not affected by the latter's doings. The body is reborn a number of times according to its Karma and goes through life and death as per the Supreme Will. If this is so, then who goes to hell or heaven?

The real experiencer of anything, in an individualistic way, is neither the Self nor the physical body. It is the mind that is the centre of individuality, that individualizes and imprisons a ray of the Atman in what is called the individual soul. And it is this mind, as embodied in the subtle body, that undergoes the pleasure of heaven or the pains of hell, or for that matter, any experience through a gross or a subtle body.

The mind appears to have consciousness on account of there being a ray of the Atman in it, in the form of a reflection, very much limited by its own constitution. Hence it will be clear that the individuality of a person is as much real or unreal as a reflection of a real object.

Though everything happens according to the Supreme Will, the Karma of the individual determines the form or shape of the experience that is to be had under the dispensation of this Will. It is not the Atman or the body that has any type of relative experience, though the body is a gross means of experience; it is the mind that has all this.

155

We see a very good man suffering too much. Why? The answer may be: "Because of his previous Karma in his previous Janma". This we can trace back to the day of creation.

The law of Karma is inexorable. Every one reaps the fruits of his previous births. A good man only will suffer a lot, because he is hurrying up in the spiritual march. Many of his evil Karmas have to be worked out and purged out quickly to hasten his salvation in this very birth. But, God gives him extraordinary power of endurance through His grace. An aspirant or a good man gets many difficulties and sufferings. But he rejoices even in sufferings and destitution on account of the descent of the Lord's grace. He voluntarily welcomes these sufferings. The only best thing in this world is pain or suffering, because it is the eye-opener towards God.

156

How to develop Bhakti?

By Satsang, by repeating the Lord's Name, doing Kirtan, hearing Kathas, reading the Ramayana, Bhagavata and the lives of Bhaktas—*Bhakta Vijayam* and *Bhakta Lilamrita*—Vishnu Sahasranama, Narada Bhakti Sutras and Sandilya Sutras. You must develop Vairagya. This is important. Live amidst Bhaktas. Live in Ayodhya. Respect Rama Nama. You will develop Rama Bhakti. Live in Brindavan. Study Bhagavata. Do Japa of the Dvadasakshara Mantra, *"Om Namo Bhagavate Vasudevaya"*. You will develop Krishna Bhakti.

157

This creation is the result of Isvara's **Eshana-Matra. Nothing less than or beyond that Eshana can happen. Isvara is not ordaining things all the time; else He would be too busy. This means determinism which leaves very little scope for individual effort.**

The notion that Isvara ordains things only sometimes and not always and that He would be too busy if He ordains things all the time is a puerile one. Isvara can look to everything at one stroke of His Being. There is no such thing as His 'being too busy', for He is not like man, using his senses for the purpose of acting. Isvara does not act with a changing mind as man does, for Isvara's action is inseparable from an undivided, ever-vigilant, all-powerful, all-pervading Consciousness which neither sleeps nor takes rest. Isvara is essentially this sovereign Consciousness itself. The whole universe is determined by Isvara's creative Will. But this is no determinism in the sense of a denial of free will to man. Man has a comparatively clear consciousness of himself and of others related to him outside, and he is possessed of the power of discrimination and willing. Isvara is the basis of cosmic activity as well as individual action, and yet, He is not involved in the actions of the individual. To Isvara, everything is determined. The past, the present and the future are all Isvara's Being alone. But from the individual's own limited standpoint, there is, in spite of the fact of a changeless universal law, a sort of apparent freedom of action imposed upon himself by his own individuality. Though the individual's freedom of thought and action is not the final truth about it, it assumes a relative importance and begins to affect the individual with its reactions, as a result of the individual's notion of the reality of a limited personality and its thoughts and actions. On account of this self-created bondage the Jiva suffers and this suffering comes to an end the moment the Jiva realises its identity with Isvara in consciousness, in activity and in its very existence itself.

158

Does a full-fledged Yogi not feel tempted to test his Yogic powers? Is such testing justified?

A full-fledged Yogi can never have the idea either to test himself or his powers. If such be the case, he should in no way be considered full-fledged or well-baked. It is only the raw, the ill-expanded and half-baked Sadhaks or Yogins that will have the inclination to test their own selves, i.e., their progress, by virtue of the powers they might have acquired.

Yogic powers cannot but manifest in proportion to the amount of progress one makes in Yoga as per the injunctions laid down in the Yoga Sastras; and they are surely a detriment to one's further progress if even the slightest attention is paid towards them either to advertise oneself or to test oneself. Every day, every minute, nay, every second, will see some blissful experience or the other even without the wish of the Yogic aspirant. As these experiences manifest of their own accord, the aspirant is to remain indifferent and unconcerned and wonder at the glory of glorious God; and he should not care to have even a knowledge of the experiences. Only then, and then alone, can he be expected to have onward progress. A full-fledged Yogi is he who has attained Self-realisation through the medium of Yoga and so there can never be any temptation in him to know who he is or how far he has progressed by dint of the powers acquired.

159

How does a person feel when he severs, all of a sudden, all relationships with this mundane world for embracing Sannyas?

When there is a true spirit of Tyaga in any, there can never be any idea of the old impressions of the world or of past relations with mundane existence. Even if the person embraces Sannyas without the indispensable Vairagya, he need not necessarily feel for the loss that he sustains, though the latent Vasanas, Vrittis and Samskaras still lie embedded in his mental consciousness. A true Sannyasi enjoys the utmost bliss when he cuts asunder all connections with the world.

160

I read your writings in "My Magazine": "Woman is only a rotten leather bag containing urine, pus, wool, blood, etc." How can we condemn and deprecate womankind? I think that there is nothing unholy in this universe.

Too much study and a little practice bring bewilderment. To induce Vairagya in the passionate people, I place such a negative mental picture of women. Really, women are manifestations of Sakti. Yes, all is holy. All is sacred. All is beautiful. This can be realised and felt only by people advanced in the spiritual line. Beginners can merely repeat these formulas like a parrot. Their experience, Drishti and mode of Sadhana are entirely different from the expressions of realised persons. Beginners should be very careful, as they will be easily duped by Maya.

161

Politics has become the God of the day and is more so in India. Religion has come to be regarded as a superfluous thing. How then is it possible to make everyone believe in God and religion?

It is wrong to regard that politics has got precedence over religion. In personal life, the majority of mankind does believe in God; and in India, there is an undercurrent of religion throughout the land. Politics is only a surface activity thrust upon most people due to socio-economic forces.

When one gets knocks and blows, when he gets disgusted with the sensual objects on account of their impermanency, when he gets experience and discrimination and dispassion, his mind will be turned towards God. Now he becomes susceptible to religious influence; and the company of good men and spiritual books make him religious. Till then there is no use of forcing religion on this man.

162

Does the soul take a new body in one year? Does it take ten years? How long does one live upon the subtler planes before reappearing on the earth plane?

There is no definite period of time in this matter. In main, two factors decide this issue, viz., the nature of the individual Karma and the last impression before death. It may vary from hundreds of years to a few months even. Those that work out some of their Karmas in other planes in subtler regions take a considerable time before entering a fresh body. The interval is very long, for a year of the earth period passes off as a single day on the celestial plane. There is an instance cited where, seeing the amazement and admiration of foreign tourists at the imposing ruins of certain ancient monuments, a saint present in the vicinity remarked that some of those very people had fashioned those monuments centuries ago.

A very sensual individual with strong craving or one with intense attachment sometimes is reborn quickly. Also in cases where life is cut short by a violent death or a sudden unexpected accident, the Jiva resumes the thread very soon. Usually, in such cases of immediate rebirth, the Jiva often remembers many of the events of its previous life. It recognizes its former relatives and friends and identifies its old home and familiar objects. This sometimes leads to very queer developments. There are some instances where a murdered person, being reborn, has declared the manner of his death and revealed the identity of the killer in the recent past.

But such cases of immediate rebirth are not common. Generally, for an average individual, the interval between death and rebirth happens to be a considerable period measured in terms of earth time. Persons who have done much good Karma spend a great deal of time on the Daivic plane before being born again. Great souls, spiritually advanced persons, wait for a long time before reincarnating.

163

What is music? Has it got any power to soothe the aching mind?

Music is a system of harmonious, melodious and rhythmic sounds capable of producing inner peace and an inexpressible thrill of joy. Music is one of the sciences which deal with Nada (Sabda) which is the first vibration of Brahman represented by the Pranava—Om. All the Sapta Svaras—Sa, Ri, Ga, Ma, Pa, Dha,

Ni—which evolved themselves later into the various vocal sounds first originated out of this fundamental Om, symbolic of Brahman. Music is one of the fine arts or Lalita Kalas. Yes. It has got not only the power to soothe the aching mind, but also the power to cure diseases like neurasthenia, insomnia, hysteria, moroseness, giddiness, etc. To achieve perfection in the Sangita Sastra is to attune oneself with Brahman. As Brahman is Light Absolute, Knowledge Absolute, Bliss Absolute and so on, so is He Nada Absolute. God is Nada Brahman. One can achieve God, even as the votaries of music, Thyagaraja, Purandhara Das, Tukaram and others, did.

164

If God ordains all, it is impossible that I can kill or steal, unless He wishes to punish my victim through me. The victim's Karmas have fructified and it is necessary that he should die, etc. If he does not get killed, the whole structure of this creation falls through. I am therefore brought in contact with the victim to carry out His behests. An executioner is paid by the Government for doing his job. Even so, why should I not be rewarded for carrying out His will, rather than be punished for doing the Papa Karma? Hitler could not have brought on war and killed so many persons. It is idle to blame him.

God is all and He alone does everything; and yet, when man feels that he is the doer, he is also the experiencer of the rewards and punishments consequent upon his actions. It is to be remembered that evil is possible only in the state of individuality or Jivahood or egoism and not when one is God-realised, God-inspired or when one is an instrument in the hands of God. The Jiva cannot think that it is expected to kill a victim and that this is sanctioned by the Will of God, for the Jiva is not omniscient and cannot know what exactly is the Will of God, unless it is raised to the state of being in tune with God. No Jiva should fall into the misconception that it is meant to exhaust the Karmas of the victim by killing the victim. This foolish act will react upon the person who commits the action and the result will be intense suffering to the person responsible for this deed.

God does not directly speak to any Jiva and say that it should kill or steal, and if the Jiva falls into the error of committing these actions, it alone is responsible, and not God. There is no such thing as God's directing an individual to perpetrate evil, commit murder or indulge in any kind of violence or do anything which is against others' well-being. All such misdeeds are the outcome of ignorance and delusion and one who does these is punished by retributive justice. Divine activity is always a movement towards freedom, perfection, peace and bliss, and it will not be in any way a cause of even the slightest suffering or pain.

165

Can I have mental Shanti and can I feel the spiritual vibrations if I come to Rishikesh?

Yes. You can. When you come here, come alone. If you come here with your company of friends, you will create the same worldly atmosphere with all sorts of talks. Come and have the Darshan of Mahatmas. Hear their spiritual instructions. Live with them. Observe

Mouna and practise concentration and meditation. Then only will you enjoy peace.

166

I am retired from service. I have fixed up my sons in service. What should I do now to lead the life of a Yogi?

Moha is very difficult to eradicate. It is a strong weapon of Maya. It is Moha that creates the idea of 'mineness' and the feeling of egoism. It creates infatuated love for children. You have not destroyed Moha in your heart of hearts. Cut off all connection with your wife, children, friends and relatives. Do not write letters. Go in for a Yatra and visit the Mahatmas in the places of pilgrimage. Develop Vairagya. You have found out from your own experience that you cannot get supreme peace and happiness in the worldly life. If you really have no Moha and if you have a strong desire to become a Sannyasin, then become a Sannyasin. Lead a glorious life of renunciation and attain Self-realisation by the practice of Yoga. From the experience of your Yatra, select a Guru who will guide you and follow his instructions implicitly.

167

Can I take Sannyas when I have my wife and young children? Is it not a sin to avoid these dependants when they are in a helpless condition?

If you have intense and real Vairagya born of Viveka and if you have strong Titiksha and Mumukshutva, you can take Sannyas. The Srutis declare: "Renounce the world on the very day you get Vairagya".

If you have Moha for your wife and children, you cannot get any spiritual progress, as your mind will be always thinking of them. Therefore, destroy Moha first. Possess real Vairagya.

When you are in the world, do a lot of Japa and meditation. When you advance a bit, go to a far-off place, live in seclusion, see the strength of your mind and see if you still have any Moha lurking in your mind. Then you can take Sannyas. You will get success.

Before you renounce, see that your wife and children are well-provided. Otherwise, they will constantly be thinking of you and you will be drawn by their mental currents. When you live with your wife, teach her the importance of Sannyas and ask her to do Japa and meditation. She must lead a spiritual life. Then only she will not interfere with you after your Sannyas.

Bhartrihari, Gauranga, Sadasiva Brahman and others deserted their wives. After their Sannyasa, they did not think of their wives. Did they not attain Self-realisation? Did any sin or curse touch them? Even if you do not provide for your family well, you can take Sannyas if you have real Vairagya. Just isolate yourself from your family and see whether your children are looked after or not. Ram Tirth left his wife with two young children without providing anything. But his elder son became an engineer and the other a professor. Have perfect faith in God.

168

The mind is fickle in me and the flesh is weak. Attempts at concentration are sometimes successful, but often end in disappointment. Kindly help me.

First of all, take care of your health. Become strong by proper food and mild exercises of Asan and Pranayam. Observe Brahmacharya. Then destroy desires, worries, anxieties, building castles and vicious qualities. Lead a contented life. Reduce your Vyavahara. Live in a spiritual atmosphere like in Haridwar, Rishikesh, Uttarkashi, etc. Observe Mouna for full three months. You can easily control the mind.

169

I feel a burning sensation in my eyes and my mind is restless; and so I am unable to meditate. Is there any effective remedy?

It is a sign to show that your system is heated. Apply Amalaka oil or butter to the head for fifteen minutes in the early morning and then take a bath. Take Sattvic food. Whenever you feel thirsty, drink a cup of Misri Sharbat (water in which sugar-candy is dissolved). Take a cup of pure cow's milk in the early morning and at night before going to bed. Regulate your food. Take bath twice a day. That will cool the system.

170

Whenever I try to concentrate on the Trikuti, I get a slight headache. Is there any remedy?

If concentration at the Trikuti produces headache, have Nasikagra Drishti, gazing at the tip of the nose. This will relieve you. Do not struggle with your mind. Take rest for half an hour. If you still feel the headache, close your eyes and then meditate.

171

Can a man of my type at the age of 45 enter into the Hatha Yogic practices? How can I get full vigour and vitality at this stage?

Yes. You must have sincerity, earnestness, faith, vigour and vitality. You must proceed cautiously, step by step. Over-exertion should be avoided. The Yogic practices will give you success if you observe Mouna, Mitahara and practice of Japa and meditation. Success in Asan, Pranayam, etc., depends upon the constitution. There are different exercises to suit different people.

If you want vigour and vitality become a true Brahmachari from this very moment. Be established in mental and physical Brahmacharya. Take Sattvic food. Develop Vairagya. Study my book "Practice of Brahmacharya". You will find practical exercises there for keeping up Brahmacharya.

172

How can I find out if I have got Chitta Suddhi or not?

Sexual thoughts, worldly desires, unholy ideas, sexual Vasanas, anger, vanity, hypocrisy, egoism, greed, jealousy, etc. will not arise in your mind if you have Chitta Suddhi. You will have no attraction for sensual objects. You will have sustained and lasting Vairagya. Even in dreams you will not entertain evil thoughts. You will possess all the virtuous divine qualities such as mercy, cosmic love, forgiveness, harmony and balance of mind. These are the signs to indicate that you have attained Chitta Suddhi.

173

The Hindus worship the phallus or the sex organ. They are ignorant people. They have no philosophy.

This is the sarcastic statement of a curious, passionate, impure foreigner of little understanding or intelligence. When a foreigner tries to learn the Tamil or the Hindustani language, he first tries to pick up some vulgar words. This is his curiosity nature. Even so, the curious foreigner tries to find out some defects in the worship of symbols. The Linga is only the outward symbol of the formless being, Lord Siva.

Linga means 'mark' in Sanskrit. It is a symbol which points to an inference. When you see a big flood in a river, you infer that there must have been heavy rains the previous day. When you see smoke, you infer that there must be fire. This vast world of countless forms is a Linga of the omnipotent Lord. The Siva Linga is a symbol of Lord Siva. When you look at the Linga, your mind is at once elevated and you begin to think of the Lord.

There is a mysterious power or indescribable Sakti in the Linga to induce concentration of the mind. Just as the mind is focussed easily in crystal gazing, so also, it attains one-pointedness when it looks at the Lingam. That is the reason why the ancient Rishis of India have prescribed the Lingam for being installed in the temples of Lord Siva.

To a sincere devotee, the Linga is not a block of stone. It is all radiant Tejas or Chaitanya. The Linga talks to him, makes him shed profuse tears, produces horripilation and melting of the heart. It raises the devotee above body-consciousness and helps him to commune with the Lord and attain Nirvikalpa Samadhi. Lord Rama worshipped the Siva Linga at Rameswar. Ravana, the learned scholar, worshipped the golden Linga. What a lot of mystic Sakti there should be in the Linga!

The light of consciousness manifesting out of Sadasiva is, in reality, the Siva Linga. From Him all the moving and unmoving creations take their origin. He is the Linga or cause of everything. In Him the whole world merges itself finally. The Siva Purana says: *"Pitham Ambamayam Sarvam Sivalingascha Chinmayam"*. The support or Pitham of all is Prakriti or Parvati; and the Linga is Chinmaya Purusha, the Effulgent Light which is self-luminous. The union of Prakriti and Purusha, of Parvati and Siva Linga, is the cause of the world.

The union of Linga with Yoni is a representation of the eternal union between the static and the dynamic aspects of the Absolute Reality. This represents the eternal spiritual communion of the paternal and the maternal principles from which all the phenomenal diversities have originated. This is an eternal communion of the changeless Being and the dynamic Power or Sakti from which all changes flow.

The lower sexual propensities in the aspirants are eradicated by this sublime conception. The spiritualization and divinization of Linga and Yoni help the aspirants to free themselves from sexual thoughts. All base thoughts gradually vanish by entertaining this lofty idea. All sexual relations in this world are spiritualized as the manifestations of the ultimate Creative Principle, of the eternal self-enjoyment and self-multiplication of Lord Siva in and through His Power or Sakti.

174

What is the easiest way for concentration?

Japa of the Name of the Lord. And a very important point to bear in mind in this connection is that perfect concentration is not achieved in just a day; you should never despair and give up your efforts. Be calm. Be patient. Do not worry yourself if the mind wanders. Be regular in your Japa; stick to the meditation hour. Slowly the mind will automatically turn Godward. And once it tastes the bliss of the Lord, nothing will be able to shake it.

175

Why do we not remember our past lives?

Such remembrance under our existing limitations would considerably complicate our present life. Therefore, the wise and beneficent Lord has so ordered our mental evolution that we cannot recall our past lives until such time as it is good and helpful for us to remember. Such instances may well form a cycle which is all clear to us when we come to the end of it, when we see a whole rosary of lives threaded upon the one personality.

176

It has been said against reincarnation that there are more people now in comparison with the past world population.

It is not necessary that the same persons are reborn into this earth and none else. In the process of evolution into human life, many from lower births also come up to the human level. All these are controlled by superhuman powers or by the Divinity, God or Isvara Himself. Further, rebirth need not necessarily be on this earth plane alone. It can take place anywhere in the universe.

177

I am observing fast on Ekadasi days. I hear that fasting will cut short the life of man. Is it a fact?

Certainly not. By fasting, the body, mind, Prana and nerves will be renovated, vivified. All the impurities will be destroyed. One can develop easily Sattvic qualities. The mind becomes calm and peaceful. All the diseases can be destroyed by fasting. If a glutton takes to fasting, he will find it difficult. A man of Mitahara will take great pleasure in fasting. He can live for a longer period. Constant fasts for long periods should be avoided. Gradual practice is necessary. In the beginning, observe fast for a day in a month. Then, once in fifteen days. After some time, you can fast once a week.

178

In the last eight years, I have spent my days in studying the Vichar Sagar, Panchadasi, Gita, Upanishads, etc., and I have mastered them in a way. But I do not *feel* the oneness of life in all. Are the scriptures for mere study alone?

Mere study of the Vichar Sagar or Panchadasi cannot bring in the experience of pure Advaitic consciousness. Vedantic gossiping and dry discussions on scriptures cannot help a man in feeling the unity and oneness of life. You should destroy ruthlessly all sorts of impurities, hatred, jealousy, envy, idea of superiority and all barriers that separate man from man. This can be done by incessant, selfless service of humanity with the right mental attitude. Practical Vedanta is rare in these days. There are dry discussions and meaningless fights over the nonessentials of religions. People study a few books and pose as Jivanmuktas. Even if there be one real Jivanmukta, he will be a great dynamic force to guide the whole world. He can change the destiny of the world. The present-day Jivanmuktas are mere bookworms. Many imagine that they can become Jivanmuktas by a little study of Laghu Siddhanta Kaumudi and Tarka. Oneness of life can be had only by Self-realisation through constant spiritual practice. Study of scriptures can help you a bit, but it cannot make you a Jivanmukta.

179

In spite of my thorough search, I am not in a position to find out a real Guru. Can you suggest one?

To find out a real Guru who may sincerely look after the disciple is a very difficult task in this world. It is quite true. But, to find out a true disciple who may sincerely follow the instructions of a Guru is indeed a very, very difficult task in this world. Have you thought over this point? Do not use your reason too much in the selection of a Guru. If you fail to get a Guru of the first-class type, try to get one who is treading the spiritual path for some years, who has right conduct and other virtuous qualities, and some knowledge of the scriptures. Just as a Sub-assistant Surgeon will be able to attend on a patient when the Civil Surgeon is not available, so also, the second-class type of Guru will be of great help to you in the absence of a first-class Guru.

180

Is it absolutely necessary for a Sannyasin to wear coloured cloth?

The glory and liberty of a Sannyasin can hardly be imagined by the householders. If there is a change inside the mind, there must be a change outside also. Wearing the ochre-coloured cloth, the orange robe, is very necessary for one who has a changed mind. Due to the force of Maya or habit, when the senses go to the objects of enjoyment, the moment you look at the coloured cloth you wear, it will remind you that you are a Sannyasin. It will give you a kick and save you from vicious actions. It has got its own glory and advantages. A real Sannyasin only can cut off all connections and ties and completely get rid of Moha. His friends and relatives will not trouble him. The robe is of great service when one appears on the platform for preaching. It has got its own sanctity in the minds of Hindus. The common people will receive the ideas more readily from Sannyasins.

181

In your book "Easy Steps to Yoga", you speak about the importance of Brahmacharya. I get tired after the day's hard labour; is it a sin to look at my wife who gives me pleasure? Does Brahmacharya help one escape

old age? The sexual act is necessary for renewing life. All man's mental powers give him no chance of escaping the time-linked process of birth, life, ageing and death. For the propagation of the species, man and woman have been provided with this creative power; and the sex act is a necessity.

You have viewed the topic from a thoroughly wrong angle. The very premise for your theory is wrong. Immortality does not pertain to the physical body. Once born, a man has to die, i.e., cast off the physical body. That state in which you freely enjoy the continuity of life without entering the cycle of birth and death is immortality. Unless you identify yourself with that Cosmic Self which transcends all limitations of space and time, you cannot enjoy immortality. To identify and realise that Immortal Self, you should conserve and preserve every bit of the energy within you. There is only one energy within us which is able to do the different functions under various forms. As you expect a long life to the machines you use by keeping them in a good condition and doing the minimum work without allowing them either to rust or to waste, you should maintain this body well-conditioned and have its life prolonged by preserving the energy within. Without the body, how can you probe into the higher planes?

Please go through my translation of the Srimad Bhagavad Gita. Practise the sort of renunciation advocated by it. It does not require you to renounce family life. You have to live in the world and learn through the world without becoming one of the world. Your duty is to maintain the household, but not to get attached to it. Then and then alone will you have that purity of mind which will enable you to progress on your path towards the attainment of perennial peace, joy and bliss.

Enough of your wrong notions. Awake and understand your true imperishable nature. Behold your true immortal, all-pervading Self and rest in it drinking the nectar of immortality. Follow my instructions. You will be a thoroughly changed personality with inner spiritual strength. Have faith and sincerity. Success is yours. Thou art That.

182

Is it absolutely necessary to do Nishkama Karma Yoga for Self-realisation? If so, how should it be done?

Yes. You cannot understand and realise the spirit and object of Vedanta if you neglect to practise Nishkama Karma Yoga for the eradication of the impurities in the mind. Nishkama Karma Yoga gives you Chitta Suddhi and eventually culminates in the realisation of the unity of the Self.

Serve everyone with intense love, without the idea of agency, without expectation of fruits, reward or appreciation. Feel that you are only a Nimitta or an instrument in the hands of God. Worship God in the poor and the sick. Have no attachment to any place, person or thing. Keep up mental poise amidst the changes of the world without consideration of success or failure, gain or loss, pleasure and pain. Have the mind always rooted in the Self amidst activities. Then you will become a true Karma Yogi. Work elevates, when done in the right spirit. Even if people scoff at you, beat and kill you, be indifferent. Continue your Sadhana.

183

The mistakes and sins in my life are countless and the limit of my ignorance is infinite. I have not learnt Sanskrit. Kindly let me know if I can tread the path of spirituality.

Ignorance is a mental Kalpana, imagination. Thou art an embodiment of wisdom. When the veil drops, you will shine in your own Svarupa. Allow the Vasanas and egoism to pass. Break the clouds. Behind the clouds, there is the luminous sun. Behind the mind, there is the self-radiant Atman. Purify yourself. Destroy the evil Vrittis. Plod on in the spiritual path. You have taken this life for this purpose only. For Self-realisation and the spiritual path, Sanskrit is not at all necessary. You will have to understand the theory and essence only. All the Sanskrit books are rendered into English and other languages. Be not troubled on this score. Sanskrit may help you a bit. That is all. If you find time, you can learn the alphabets so that you can read some Stotras, Gita Slokas and the Upanishads.

184

Should it not be considered as Himsa when we cut vegetables and fruits?

Cutting vegetables is not Himsa. There is no real consciousness in plants and trees, although there is life in them. There is life in plants, sensation in animals, mentality in human beings and spirituality in sages. There is no Visesha Ahankara and reflection of Chaitanya in plants and trees. Hence they cannot experience pain. The tree will not say, "I am experiencing pain". The mind in plants and trees is not developed. It is quite rudimentary. It is Jada and insentient. Life on earth will be impossible if we take cutting vegetables also as Himsa. This is only splitting the hairs. This is the idle philosophy of those who take interest in vain discussions and arguments. Ignore trifles. Become a practical man.

185
Why does God not speak to me? What is the obstacle?

The self-surrender is not complete. There are still subtle Moha, subtle desires and egoism. The Indriyas are still powerful and outgoing. These are the obstacles. When these are removed, you can hear the shrill, sweet, inner voice of God. Impure souls mistake the voice of the impure mind for the voice of God.

186
I am disgusted with the false world. I know fully well that it is no use living in such a world. Everywhere I find misery alone. I intend to enter into the life of a Sannyasin, but I do not know where to find out a Guru. Kindly let me know what I have to do to become a Sannyasin.

You should not hate the world, but you should hate the worldly life. The world is a manifestation of the Lord. The world is the best teacher for you. The world cannot stand in the way of your attainment of Kaivalya. You must change the way of your living and viewing things. You will have to build a new mind and a new vision. Then the world will appear as heaven. You have not developed real Vairagya. It is a kind of temporary aversion on account of some mishap. You are unfit for taking Sannyas. You may fail to carry out the duties of a Sannyasin. You must ascend the spiritual ladder step by step.

I will advise you to remain in the world and do Nishkama Karma Yoga for some years to purify the heart (Chitta Suddhi). You must develop humility, the spirit of self-sacrifice, Kshama, mercy, Visva-prem. These virtues can be acquired by selfless service alone. You must have the qualifications Sama (peaceful nature), Dama (self-restraint), Sarva-sanga-parityaga (freedom from all sorts of attachments), and perfect obedience to and implicit faith in the teacher before you approach a Guru for taking Sannyas. Otherwise you will not be benefited.

187

When I know that this world is not real and I am bound to leave it one day or the other, why should I not renounce it now? Taking Pati Seva as my duty, I am doing it very sincerely and faithfully. But I know that neither Pati nor son nor father nor mother can help me in achieving the real goal. Did not Mira meet Bhagavan by leaving her husband?

For a lady, her husband is the image of God. She will have to realise God in and through him alone. She need not go to temples even for worship. Your Vairagya is a momentary bubbling. It cannot help you in any way in your spiritual progress. You may say, "This world is unreal"; but in your heart of hearts you may be attached to several objects. The Vairagya that comes temporarily out of family difficulties and troubles is like a flash of lightning. It will pass away in no time.

In what sense is the world unreal? The world is not as unreal as the horn of a hare or the son of a barren woman. This world is an empirical or relative reality (Vyavaharic Satta). It is not so real as Brahman. When compared with Brahman or the Eternal, it has no real existence. The world is a phenomenon or an appearance. Brahman is the noumenon or the absolute. The world is unreal only for a Jnani who is resting in his own Svarup. The vast majority of persons have misunderstood the term 'Mithya'. Hence they try to leave the world aimlessly without any discipline and without developing any virtue. This is a sad mistake. Taking the world as a mere appearance, you will have to work in the world with untiring patience without egoism, but with Atma Bhav and with a clear understanding of the noumenon or the basis of the world. If the aspirant leaves the world without purification of the heart through Nishkama Karma Yoga and without possessing the four means of salvation, he will not be benefited in the least by his renunciation.

The case of Mira is quite different. She was a Yoga-Brashta with full Vairagya, with a heart saturated with Krishna-prem from her very childhood. Your case is different. Do not draw a comparison here. You will have to evolve through serving your husband and humanity. Practise this. See the Lord Krishna in the sparkling eyes of your husband and in all faces. May God bless you!

188

I have no desire to leave Grihastha life at this moment and yet I am very, very keen to awaken the Kundalini Sakti. Is this possible? Will Your Holiness help me?

Yes, you can stick to Grihastha Ashrama. But live as an ideal householder. Support the other three Ashramas. If the duties of a householder are strictly followed, there is no necessity for Sannyas.

Become a true Brahmachari and give up sexual intercourse completely. You have enough children. The practice of Yoga strictly demands this from you if you desire to make real, substantial, rapid spiritual progress. Train your wife also in the spiritual path. Let her also repeat the same Mantra you are repeating and study religious books and observe occasional fasts or live on milk and fruits.

You can continue Sirshasan as usual. Observe strictly the rules of right conduct. Be established in the practice of Yama and Niyama. Purify your heart first before you awaken the Kundalini. Remove completely jealousy, selfishness, anger, lust, Moha, pride, Raga and Dvesha. Then Kundalini can be easily awakened. Yes. It is quite possible for you to awaken the Kundalini. I shall help you in its awakening. Don't worry. Increase your Japa and meditation. You can achieve spiritual success by remaining as a Grihastha, but you must be a true Brahmachari in thought, word and deed.

189

Your Holiness advises a man to treat his wife as "World Mother" as soon as a son is born to him. In case

the son dies after a few months, there will be no heir left to look after his estate. Under such circumstances, what should he do? Kindly let me have your advice.

Why should you bother about heir for the estate? Did you bring the estate with you? Would you take it also when you die? What is estate? Is it not a lump of earth only? Can this estate and heir give you happiness and peace? Are they not sources of misery and worry? The desires for property and children will bind a man to the wheel of Samsara. These are all hindrances for a Jijnasu.

What did Lord Buddha and Bhartrihari do with their estates? Did each one crave for a son to look after his estate? How can a man who thinks of property and son think of God? It is impossible to think of God and Mammon. In the presence of light, darkness cannot exist. When you enjoy sensual pleasure, you cannot have the bliss of Atma.

If you beget another child, you will multiply your miseries. You have already many ties around your neck. He who has rightly understood the magnitude of human sufferings will never bring forth a child into the world. If your mind is full of Vasanas and if you find it difficult to curb the passions, you can have a second son. Then become a true Brahmachari.

190

God is all-pervading formless Being. How can He be confined to an idol? What is the use of idol worship?

The divinity of the all-pervading God is vibrant in every atom of creation. There is not a speck of space where He is not. Why do you then say that He is not in the idols?

The idol is a support for the neophyte. It is a prop of his spiritual childhood. A form or image is necessary for worship in the beginning. It is not possible for all to fix the mind on the Absolute or the Infinite. A concrete form is necessary for the vast majority for practising concentration.

Idols are not the idle fancies of sculptors, but shining channels through which the heart of the devotee flows towards God. Though the image is worshipped, the devotee feels the presence of the Lord in it and pours out his devotion unto it. The idol remains an idol, but the worship goes to the Lord.

To a devotee, the image is a mass of Chaitanya or consciousness. He draws inspiration from the image. The image guides him. It talks to him. It assumes human form to help him in a variety of ways. The image of Lord Siva in the temple at Madurai in South India helped the fuel-cutter and the old woman. The image in the temple at Tirupati assumed human form and gave witness in the court to help His devotees. There are marvels and mysteries. Only the devotees understand these.

Idol worship is not peculiar to Hinduism. The Christians worship the Cross. They have the image of the Cross in their mind. The Mohammedans keep the image of the Kaaba stone when they kneel and do prayers. The mental image also is a form of idol. The difference is not one of kind, but only one of degree.

All worshippers, however intellectual they may be, generate a form in the mind and make the mind dwell on that image. Everyone is an idol worshipper. Pictures and drawings are only a form of Pratima. A gross mind needs a concrete symbol as a prop or Alambana; a subtle mind requires an abstract symbol. Even a Vedantin has the symbol OM for fixing the wandering mind. It is not only pictures or images in stone and wood that are idols. Dialectics and leaders also become idols. So, why condemn idolatry?

191

Is woman made for man and to serve him only? Did God create us for the kitchen and for procreation? Why should a woman play a secondary part? Why do you deny equal rights to women?

Woman is in no way inferior to man. The home is a cooperative organization. It flourishes on the principle of division of labour. If a man earns and the wife stays at home, it does not mean that the woman is a parasite and a slave. She is indeed the builder of the nation. To make noble citizens by training their children and to form the character of the whole human race is undoubtedly a power far greater than that which women could hope to exercise as voters or law-makers, as presidents, ministers or judges.

The idea that men and women are equals is purely a Western concept. The Indian or Hindu concept is that man and woman, Purusha and Sakti, are one and indivisible. Sita did not think herself as a separate entity. She was in and of Rama. The Indian woman always identifies herself completely with her husband in all domestic, religious and social life. She is the queen of the house. She illumines the home through the glory of motherhood. It is in the motherhood of woman that all her prerogative, glory, competency and jurisdiction are specially vested.

The West has seen women playing the man in every walk of life. But I ask: "Has this contributed more to human happiness and to the real prosperity and peace of the country? Surely it has brought more divorce courts, more unhappiness, more restlessness. This has only thickened the women's veil of ignorance and augmented their Rajasic element".

Even in the West, there are many persons who are not in favour of women claiming equality with men. Even those who were in favour of this movement are now seriously repenting for their wrong advocacy, because they are actually witnessing before their eyes its pernicious effects.

Loose life is not perfect freedom. Promiscuous mixing is not freedom. Some women of India have ruined themselves by taking advantage of this false freedom.

The ideal of the woman in the West should not be our ideal, for then we shall not only be denaturalized, but also denationalised. One nation cannot adopt the ideal and the social customs of another without undermining one's own rock-bottom base.

Women should become good mothers only. This is the function they will have to perform in the grand plan of God. This is what is meant in the divine plan. This is the will of God. Women have their own psychological traits, temperament, capacities, virtues, instincts and impulses. They have their own disadvantages in society. They cannot, and should not, compete with men.

192

Is married life not an obstruction to God-realisation? How can a married man please both his wife and God simultaneously?

Married life can never be an obstruction to those who are endowed with dispassion and detachment to worldly objects and who consider that life is intended to mould one's own self by drawing lessons from the university of Nature. Study the lives of saints like Thyagaraja, Ekanath, Narsi Mehta, Bhadrachalam Ramdas, Tukaram, Namdev, Jayadeva, Chaitanya and Kabir. Probe deep into the world and the way in which the above-mentioned saints and a host of others actually led their lives.

It is disgraceful on the part of man if he tries to please himself by pleasing his wife. He who considers married life as intended to please his wife is worse than an abject slave. Be self-restrained. Let the wife be made aware of the aim and purpose of life and the ways and means of attaining it in and through Grihastha life. Do not yield to the lower impulses when prompted by your incorrigible nature or by the stubborn character of the other party, but arrange yourself in such a balanced way that the psychic and physical personality of neither is upset. Whatever actions you do, dedicate them to God and consider them not as yours. Pray for a self-purifying, contented and continent life. Resign yourself recklessly in the spiritual battlefield and make no retreat even if life happens to be at stake. Be a master over yourself and treat yourself as a servant of God, but not as a servant of your wife. Feign that you are one with your wedded partner, but be ever transcending in mental outlook. You can be on the safe side of life.

193

Shall I do Japa of "Om Narayana" instead of "Om" in order to make it both Nirguna and Saguna? Japa of the Narayana Mantra keeps the Chaturbhuj Murti of the Lord before my mental eyes. I, however, have been accustomed to meditate on the Murti of Lord Krishna and am in search of a Chaturbhuj Murti of Lord Krishna with Arjun at His feet. Please let me know how I should go on in future.

You have already created a clear mental image, momentum and force by meditating on Lord Krishna. It is not good to change the form now. Even if you change it, the old form will come before the mind through force of habit. Therefore, have the same image only. Do not go in for Lord Krishna with four hands.

Om Narayana is not the proper Mantra. The proper Mantra is *Om Namo Narayanaya*.

Om is both Saguna and Nirguna. If you study Prasnopanishad, you will understand this point well.

If at all you wish to change the Mantra, you can revert to *Om Namo Bhagavate Vasudevaya*. You can repeat this for some time.

194

I have been reading the Upanishads and other scriptures and I find one and the same thing in all of them. They say that everything we come across is unreal, only God is real and that we have to think and

understand the Truth by ourselves. How are we to do it, Swamiji?

Reading will help you only to a certain extent. Too much reading will land you in confusion. You should meditate and concentrate on one particular idea. That particular idea should serve as the eye-opener. Then alone will you get Vairagya; you will be able to understand the false nature of things. Take, for instance, the life of Sri Swami Sadasiva Brahmendra of Nerur. The mere uttering of the word 'wait' by his mother, when he asked her to serve food, inflicted such a blow on his mind and stirred it so well as to make him understand the Reality.

You may be convinced intellectually that the world is false, only God is real and all the sense-enjoyments bring misery only. But this conviction is not strong. You may think, "Let me enjoy the sense-pleasures for five minutes". Thus you are deceived by Maya. All sense-pleasures are sugar-coated pills made by Maya. You must reflect on such Slokas as *"Ye Hi Samsparsaja Bhoga Duhkha Yonaya Eva Te....".* You should identify with the Higher Self which is infinity, eternity, immortality. Always think, "Suddhoham, Shantoham, Satchidanandoham". You will be elevated. Abhyasa and Vairagya are necessary. Tyaga and Tapas will give you tremendous powers. Be not cheated by the temporary pleasures of the world—car, property etc. Be not unnecessarily worried by undue attachment etc. Do your duty and leave the rest to Him. He will take care of you.

195

Is not a realised soul selfish as he has sought his emancipation only? Also, if all renounce, what will be the result?

The question is based on a wrong hypothesis. If all the women are barren, if all turn out to be doctors or lawyers or dacoits, what would become of the world? Only a few with an accumulated wealth of spiritual Samskaras can have Vairagya and renunciation.

The saint purifies the whole world. He is not selfish. Sankara, Ramanuja and others worked for the entire mankind. Even he who lives in seclusion or leads an 'incognito' life, influences the world with his thought-currents. Even a novice in the spiritual path does great good to the world by his pure thoughts. These things, the ways and actions of saints and saintly people, cannot be understood by an impure mind.

196

Observance of Brahmacharya would appear to be meaningless, because scientists, through laboratory tests, have proved that semen cannot be reabsorbed into the system and that the brain has nothing to do with semen.

Semen is a mysterious secretion that is able to create a living body. Semen itself is living substance. It is life itself. Therefore, when it leaves man, it takes a portion of his own life. A living thing cannot be put to laboratory tests, without first killing it. The scientist has no apparatus to test it. God has provided the only test to prove its precious nature, viz., the womb. The very fact that semen is able to create life is proof enough that it is life itself.

I have thousands of letters from young men who have wasted this precious fluid and are in a miserable plight. Several young men even go to the point of committing suicide! Through reckless waste of semen, they lose all their physical, mental and intellectual faculties. Those who are perfect Brahmacharins have lustrous eyes, a healthy body and mind, and a keen, piercing intellect.

Scientists with their test tubes and balances cannot approach subtle things. No amount of dissection of the body will be able to tell you where the soul is, where life is, or where the mind is. Through the practice of Yoga, the seminal *energy*—not the gross physical semen—flows upwards and enriches the mind. This has been declared by the sages. You will have to experience it yourself.

197

Is suicide the logical conclusion for a man who has come to believe that life has no meaning for him?

Suicide is not the logical conclusion of a meaningless life, but the illogical conclusion arrived at by the thoughtless and non-discriminating mind which has failed to perceive the meaning that is in life. Suicide does not remove misery or correct defects, but leads to violent reactions later on. And the reactions will be more painful than the present condition of dissatisfactory life. Suicide is pure defeatism.

198

If escape from this world be the goal, where is the incentive for social work?

Escape from the world is not the goal, but freedom from worldliness is what is desired. Social work has got its own valuable part in life until a certain stage, though after a time it is transcended by a higher consciousness. The value of social work, however, is purely subjective. It is not that one makes himself a great reformer or a saviour of mankind, but that he offers his ego as a sacrifice at the altar of universal love and so obtains purity of mind, which is the basis of all spiritual progress. For a realised soul, however, it is an urge born out of compassion for his fellow-beings.

199

What are the methods to develop unruffled serenity and mental composure under all conditions of life? Is absolute serenity possible of attainment?

Yes. By all means. Consider yourself as dead to the world or the world as dead to you. Develop Atma Vichar Sakti. Identify not with the mind, senses and intellect or with any of the other modifications of the mind. Always be engaging yourself in the thought of the Divine. Have no thought of yourself or the surrounding world. Be absolutely indifferent to yourself, as you ought to be towards the surroundings, the various daily happenings and the worldly repercussions. Knowledge of the Self, when once attained, absolves one of all mental disruptions and psychic derangements. Where there is firm-grounded knowledge of the Self in the spiritual seeker, where there is the consciousness in him that "all indeed is Brahman, *Sarvam Khalvidam Brahma*" and that he is none other than that Supreme Brahman, and where he understands that all happenings—good, bad or mixed—are but passing phases on the screen of the world, there can never be any ill-balanced mental life.

It is the mind that is the sole cause for bondage or Moksha. The mind is the substratum behind pleasure or pain, happiness or misery, success or defeat. Rise above the pairs of opposites by resorting to a Guru and his instructions. Study the lives of saints who underwent various trials and the books by realised souls. Develop the spirit of true surrender wherein you have no thought of body or bodily needs or self-protection even in the slightest degree and wherein you forget the idea of life and death altogether. Serenity is merely mental. Therefore, cultivate mental equipoise by gaining spiritual knowledge.

200

Why is Ganges water regarded so sacred? What are the scientific or religious reasons for its water being eternally free from any sort of contamination?

Is it a fact that all sins are washed away by a dip in the Ganges?

From time immemorial, Mother Ganges has been associated with sages and saints who had found immense spiritual benefit by bathing in her waters as well as by drinking it.

Fire can burn all other things, but cannot act upon its own self. Flowing down the Himalayan ranges which contain many a rare herb that possess disinfectant power to a very high degree, Mother Ganges contains the various chemicals (found in those herbs) in a nascent condition. As such, other pollutants lose their powers to defile the Ganges when thrown into her waters. All our religious dogmas are based on sound scientific reason.

Yes, all sins are washed away by a dip in the Ganges when there is a real Bhav in your mind that you are atoning for your wrong doings.

201

Don't you believe that Naga Sadhus, when moving in public, are a standing menace to our holy culture? Have they really risen to that level as to regard this nakedness as nothing indecent and bad? Is there any spiritual significance to this nakedness of body in its totality? Kindly illumine.

Our holy culture is essentially spiritual in every respect. Only when the Spirit is forgotten, dualities like decency and indecency arise. All these dualities exist for the worldly man and not for him who tries to go beyond them and establish himself in that non-dual, differenceless state. From the spiritual viewpoint, how can you then come down to the level of finding the existence of dualities and getting affected by them?

The spiritual significance of remaining naked lies in its being a helpful factor in getting over the body-consciousness or Sarira Abhimana. The man whose mind is tainted with worldly thoughts and who is awake to the dualities will feel ashamed to present himself in his birthday robe in public. Only he who has conquered his senses and mind can roam in a state of nudity in public fearlessly and without the least emotional disturbance.

Some adopt this as a part of their Sadhana to overcome the body consciousness and such people generally avoid the crowds.

Of course, there are people who impersonate realised sages and move about duping the innocent public. But people can easily understand these pseudo-saints by their reactions and hence shun them.

202

On what grounds do you prohibit meat-eating?

On medical, psychological, moral and spiritual grounds. The mind is made up of the essence of the food that a man takes. Tamasic food results in a Tamasic mind. Meat is Tamasic and hence should be avoided.

When an animal is killed or butchered, a contraction of its nervous system takes place on account of fear. (And you might have felt certain disturbances in your own stomach when you have experienced fear.) This leads to the secretion of certain poisons in the liver, etc., of the animal. These poisons are cumulative in their nature and are never removed or lost during the process of boiling or cooking meat. Hence, meat-eating is poisonous and dangerous in the long run.

There is no difference between you and an animal when both are considered as souls inhabiting the bodies. From whichever source you derive the right to live and enjoy in this material body, from that very same source, the souls of these animals have derived equal rights to live and enjoy in their material bodies. Hence, you do not possess the moral right to kill a single living being, however small it may be.

Last, but not the least, there is One Consciousness which has expressed itself in the form of the various beings, animate and inanimate. And this makes you one with all beings. When you have known this, will you consciously hurt any being? Can you willingly and joyously cut your own fingers and cook them and eat them? Knowing this oneness alone is the purpose of your coming again and again into the mundane plane. You can know, feel and experience this oneness only when you stop injuring and hurting others and begin to love all as your own Self. Verily, the animals are thy own Self. Thou alone art residing in these animals as the individual souls and thou alone art manifest in the form of the material bodies in which these souls reside. Hence, wake up; stop meat-eating and butchering the animals. Develop love for them and promote oneness.

203

Some people have alarmed me that Pranayam and Sirshasan are dangerous sometimes and it might turn a person mad even. Though I discount such alarms, yet my conviction is not firm. Kindly write of any possible harm accruing from the practice of Pranayam and Sirshasan.

Be within your limits while performing Asans and Pranayam. Do not strain yourself to the point of exhaustion. None turns mad by performing Sirshasan and Pranayam. There is a rule for everything. Start from the initial stages and gradually increase the period as you find improvement.

204

Which Yogic Asans can a married lady having children profitably practise without any harm accruing therefrom?

A Grihini with children can practise all the Asans subject to certain restrictions just as in the case of a man. She should not practise during the period of monthly courses and three or four days thereafter, during any of the ailments peculiar to her sex, and during pregnancy. Sirshasan, Sarvangasan, Matsyasan, Halasan, Padahastasan, Bhujangasan, Salabhasan and Paschimottanasan are a few of the important Asans she can practise. To these can be added Yoga Mudra and Viparitakarani Mudra. Kriyas and Bandhas, as also Surya Namaskaras, can be performed likewise. The only conditions necessary, though not compulsory, for deft performance of all these are slimness of body and balance over the physical frame. There is absolutely no harm in a household lady practising Asans, but she should subject herself to the imposed restrictions cited above.

205

What is meant by "killing of conscience"?

He who is pure in thought, speech and action, who fears sin and Adharma, who is pious, God-fearing and equanimous, who is balanced and capable of maintaining equilibrium, will have his conscience in an unblemished state. He who has abundant Sattva (quality of purity) will always have an unmarred and uncharred conscience. Expansion of heart gives rise to the hearing of the voice of conscience. Inner guidance will always be to that individual who has Sattva in abundant measure by way of Japa, Svadhyaya, Pranayam, selfless service and other elevative works (Yajna).

"Killing of conscience" means killing of what is divine in man, killing of the enviable quality of Sattva, expenditure of the laudable wealth of Dharma, the praiseworthy treasure of spiritual progress. He who is God-fearing can never commit anything that debases him or degrades him in moral evolution. To kill the conscience means to kill the God in man, to make an end of all Daivi Sampat (wealth of divine qualities) and equal oneself to a brute and reduce oneself to a spiritual cannibal. True conscience is another name for the Antaratma or Inner Soul. Go through my book "Ethical Teachings" in this connection.

206

Is procreation a sin?

Neither manhood nor womanhood nor procreation is a sin. A seeker after Truth can beget children and later take to the path of renunciation either in and through the world or entirely out of the clutches of the world. The moment one begets a male child for the upkeep of the progeny, one can devote oneself wholeheartedly to Sannyasa if he so wishes, though it is not a hard and fast rule to have a male child before taking Sannyas. The need for a male child, though not imperative, is in consonance with the Sruti.

207

How can a married man practise Brahmacharya? Is it possible especially when the couple are young?

To live and enjoy Grihastha life with one's own wife during the Ritu period subject to the imposed restrictions of the Sastras is itself Brahmacharya. Sastras say that the married man should not indulge in sense-satisfaction as and when his senses prompt him to do so. He should subject himself to the various restrictions imposed even on the enjoyment of sense life. For details in this respect, study my book, "Advice to Women". One who observes these Sastraic injunctions and leads a happy, well-regulated life is a perfect Brahmachari, though technically a Grihastha. Whatever be the natural ebullient impulses of the couple, and however young they be, it is quite possible to observe Brahmacharya on the above lines. Brahmacharya for a Grihastha does not mean absolute abstention from enjoying the conjugal life; but means a well-disciplined, self-restrained, Dharmic life.

208

Is conscience not the mode by which we can listen to the inner Atman?

The pure conscience itself is the "Inner Voice". But the difficulty in the ordinary man is that the voice of the lower mind, the voice of the brutal instincts, is often misunderstood as the voice of conscience. As a result of such misunderstanding, guided by his animal tendencies, he commits colossal blunders, involving danger to others. It requires a great degree of purity and calmness of mind to hearken the true Inner Voice.

209

May I know if you mean by 'Sastras' the age-old, written or unwritten, set and rigid principles of ancient

Hindu religious scriptures? Have these principles not become time-barred due to the fast-changing conditions? I don't think any rigid principle can stand the test of time.

Yes, the age-old, written or unwritten set principles of the ancient Hindu religious scriptures are termed 'Sastras'. But because of this, it need not follow that they should become time-barred. The fundamental tenets of right living are unchanging. There cannot be any sort of difference in the fundamentals.

Modifications, alterations and adjustments are necessary; but these should be effected in the external modes of interpretation and methods of application to suit the changing times and the new environments of a new generation.

There is no harm in changing the externals so long as it does not affect the fundamental principles. Fundamental virtues like truth, fellowship, non-injury, purity, justice, integrity, etc., will continue to be applicable to the life of humanity. Violation of these would always be a signal for coming calamity.

210

Should the means to achieve good ends be always good? Medicine tastes bitter, but cures diseases. Arjuna fought against the Kauravas to achieve good ends.

Indian thought has no hesitation in answering this question in the affirmative. Except the rank materialists, the Charvakas, the founders of all other systems of Indian thought boldly declare that "one should not adopt a foul means to achieve a desired end, however covetable that end may be". There should not be any doubt regarding this point.

I don't think that your two examples are strong enough to prove that the end justifies the means. For, the medicine, whether it be sweet or bitter, in so far as it does not do any harm to the patient or anybody else while curing the disease, should be considered as a means free from any fault. It is a fair means to achieve the end, viz., cure of the disease.

In the second example, Arjuna fought the Kauravas and killed them all, no doubt. But the battle fought by Arjuna was not an exhibition of cruelty, but an execution of one's own duty. The war fell to his lot as pure duty or Svadharma. Arjuna did not want it himself. He did not impose it on the Kauravas. He was challenged to it by them. He had to defend himself and his clan. As a Kshatriya, it was his sacred duty and moral responsibility to fight for the defence of his rights. Thus, Arjuna's fighting the battle being purely duty-bound, is thoroughly justified.

Sri Krishna has reiterated this point in several places in the Gita. On the contrary, if Arjuna had shirked away his responsibilities of fighting the battle, then he would have been failing in his Dharma. Hence the Lord's repeated commands to him: *Svadharmamapi Chavekshya Na Vikampitumarhasi* (Waver not from your own duty on seeing it in front of you), *Yudhyasva Vigatajvara* (Do thou fight, free from mental fever), etc.

211

When death is predestined and also is nothing but a pause to change the clothes, why is it, then, a sin to

commit suicide and also to kill living beings for a certain cause?

Suicide as well as killing of other beings are both considered to be great sins, as they block the course of evolution of the Jiva. Moreover, putting an end to the present gross body by force does not help one to put an end to his sufferings. Sufferings and pleasures due to him by virtue of his past actions won't leave him until and unless they are enjoyed by him completely.

On the contrary, by suicide one is inviting more miseries, for it may take some time for him to get another gross body in which he can enjoy the effects of his actions, and during this interim period, he may have to move about in the form of a Preta or ghost. It is, of course, needless to say that killing a human being is a criminal offence legally and is totally heinous from the point of view of spiritual progress, barring, of course, such contingencies as in a war.

212

Why is it that the life-span of the modern man is so short as compared to that of his ancestors?

Our ancestors used to have a well-regulated, disciplined life. They were not slaves of their senses as the modern people are. They used to do Japa, Pranayam, Sandhyavandana (Trikala) and Svadhyaya (study of religious books like the Gita, the Bhagavata and the Ramayana). They used to do charity and selfless service, and observe Vratas like Ekadasi, Sri Rama Navami, Sri Krishna Ashtami and Dattatreya Jayanti. They used to conduct spiritual conferences and pray for world peace and not for their own individual selves. They used to take plenty of physical exercise in the form of walking ten to twenty miles a day and at a stretch. They used to observe Yama and Niyama very rigidly. They used to live mostly in villages and not in congested areas. They were self-reliant and not dependent on others even for trivial matters. They used to have Kaya Siddhi as well as Vak Siddhi. When the present-day generation realises the value of the way of ancient living, surely will it achieve all that it desires with the Prasannata (grace) of the Devas.

213

What, according to you, should be the maximum number of children a spiritual-minded Grihastha should have?

Every Grihastha, be he worldly-minded or spiritually-inclined, wishes to have a son to keep up the lineage or the family line and a daughter to give an ineffable cosmic enlightenment expressive of the Divine Mother (Prakriti) who is the creatrix and origin of the universe, for it is from the womb of the Mother (Prakriti) that the entire creation is ushered into this world. No household couple is satisfied either with male issues or with female issues. They want both, to reveal themselves as the two reflections of their own individual selves, representative of Purusha and Prakriti. Besides these two—a son and a daughter—there can be one extra to avoid contingent mishaps like death and the like. A spiritually-bent householder can lead the conjugal life up to the limit of three children. Later on he can take up the Nivritti Marga for quick evolution and realisation. Study the lives of realised saints like

Tukaram, Ram Tirth and Pothana. You will understand the truth behind "realisation in and through the world". Over-indulgence in sexuality or worldly life allows no access to spiritual matters. In this connection, it is worth the remembrance that children are not an absolute necessity for realisation of Moksha, that Moksha is not debarred from those that do not beget children, and also that they are prone to exemption from the curses of the manes if they take to Sannyas without keeping up the lineage or Vamsa Vriksha.

214

Swamiji, why do you allow your feet to be worshipped, allow regular Puja to be offered to your feet?

The materialistic modern mind needs a good flushing before it can understand this. To the spiritual aspirant, the Guru's feet are not feet merely, but are the channels of divine grace. From time immemorial, the Indian seeker after truth has known that his receptive centre, viz., the head, should come into contact with the preceptor's transmitting centre, the feet, in order to get infused with spiritual power, wisdom and light. This is one of the axioms of electricity, that the positive and the negative poles should come into contact in order to complete the circuit.

Pada Puja develops the spirit of self-surrender in the aspirant. The flower symbolizing the heart, the fruits symbolizing the fruits of all actions, coins representing all wealth, and camphor symbolizing the very soul of the aspirant which gets totally absorbed in the enlightened Self of the Guru, are first offered in worship. And finally, the aspirant prostrates at the feet, signifying that everything without the least reservation is surrendered at the feet of the Satguru.

Pada Puja creates and strengthens the aspirant's faith and devotion and divine qualities like humility.

Bharata worshipped the divine feet of Lord Rama and took His sandals which he enthroned as Rama's representatives; he regarded himself as the viceroy of the sandals. It is such humility, faith and devotion that will make you divine.

Here, I do not compel people to come and worship my feet; if they, of their own accord, insist on doing so out of their Guru Bhakti towards me, I cannot refuse. If I refuse, I will not only be displeasing those who are anxious to prove their self-surrender and respect to me, but also, I will be failing in my duties. Do you think I feel happy or elevated when they do Pada Puja to me? I have to sit patiently bearing all that process. Surely it is not out of pleasure that I agree to sit patiently!!

215

What are the marks of a wise man and a fool respectively from the ultimate point of view?

The fool reacts outwardly and emotionally under all circumstances, while there is no reaction in the sage. If at all the latter acts, such actions are not reactions to any immediate action, but are born out of the sage's Satsankalpa to serve humanity. Secondly, in all situations, the fool places himself first but finds himself last, while the wise man places himself last but finds himself first. Thirdly, the wise man retires silently as soon as he has done his work, but the fool remains to hear others praise him, and in some cases, if nothing like it is coming forward, he shamelessly asks for it.

Kindly read also the Second Chapter of the Gita, wherein you will find a nice description of the Sthitaprajna.

216

Which is more powerful in human beings—hunger or the sex-urge?

The world of living beings has three things in common—Ahara (food), Nidra (sleep) and Sangama (copulation). Food (Ahara) does not play so important a part as the sex-urge in man, however much that sexual instinct develops in adolescence at the age of 16 in a male and 14 in a female. This age-limit is merely nominal and it differs in different climes and depends upon the ways and habits of the individuals. Whether a male or a female attains puberty or not, the sex instinct will ever be there by natural propensities acquired from the previous births and by witnessing common sights in the outside world. Even when a person does not take food for days together, the sexual impulses and libido will be there. Even when the sexual urge fades or dies out, either due to a far advanced age or some other reasons, the Vasana of impurity (craving for, or dreaming of, sex enjoyment) may in all likelihood still persist in the cobweb corners of the mind. At the sight of something pleasant or beautiful, the impish mind may overpower a man to recall any of the old experiences. All these clearly prove that the sex instinct is more powerful than hunger itself. Sexual hunger is simply intensified by physical hunger, as flames of fire by oblations of Ghee. Physical hunger is merely subsidiary, while sexuality is primary in the role of a man's life.

217

If a person has been forced into wedlock with a girl not at all beautiful, but abounding in qualities of head and heart, what should characterize the attitude of that man towards his wife, constantly worried as he is on the count that his wife is not beautiful? How can he manage to conceal his pent-up feelings of frustration caused by the lack of beauty in his wife—aesthetically speaking—and yet manage to lead a healthy, happy, harmonious married life?

It is not in the power of man to choose this beautiful girl or that, nor in the power of a girl to select this handsome or rich man or that. Everything is predestined. Man forgets this glaring fact, ignores this essential truth and thinks and feels that he is the real doer or the enjoyer. Say and console yourself: *"Daivadheen, Daivadheen.* Lord's Will, Lord's Will". Think and feel that everything that befalls your lot at any moment of your life is for the best. Be convinced of this grand truth and rejoice in philosophic indifference and stoic unconcernedness. Physical beauty is no beauty at all. It is skin deep. That woman who has the beauty of the virtue of chastity is the really beautiful woman on earth. This is in consonance with the proclamation of the great law-giver Manu. Study Manu Smriti, the Neeti Sastra of Manu. Hammer the mind again and again with the saying of Manu, "Chastity is the beauty of an ugly woman".

Beauty and ugliness are mental Kalpanas, illusory creations of the mind only, just as sweetness or bitterness lies in the mind and mind alone. Such are the Dharmas of the mind. Rise above the mind. Then you will be able to find beauty in ugliness, sweetness in bitterness and good in bad. Even the ideas of goodness, sweetness and beauty disappear when the proper grade of evolution is achieved.

The hand stands for Seva, the heart for Bhakti or Prem and the head for the intellect. This is a very rare combination which can be found in very few people. Beauty is the inner spirit of purity in a woman, at the very sight of which man is thrilled to horripilation and raised to heights of elysian bliss. That is to be treated as "true beauty".

Always try to see the good, the beautiful, the auspicious, the pleasant, however condemnable the worthy object of adoration be, on account of negative qualities. Then and then alone will you be able to evolve into the Infinite in greater and more abundant measure. As long as man limits himself with constricted notions and cherishes debasing, negative and dualistic thoughts, he is not to be considered as an expanded soul. Mentally prostrate before the woman who has the virtues of an Adarsha Pativrata as embodied in the epics of Bharata Varsha. Mend yourself. Feel that your position, your status, your earning capacity and your personality are but trash and a trifle when compared to the abundant wealth of beauty of solidified virtue of your wife. Give up egoistic assessment of values in life.

218

Is the cinema an evil? Does it corrupt public morals? Please explain.

Cinema, as such, is not an evil, though it generally wrecks the health of people and spoils their eyesight, when indulged in inordinately. And it leads to several evil contacts. Its great condemnation is when it consists of sensational pictures, rousing the passions, exciting the senses and causing a revolt of the immoral and non-ethical worldly propensities like lust, hatred, vanity, agitation or any form of sensuality or egoism. Of course, there is no harm in educational, religious and spiritual pictures, though there is always a tendency in men to go beyond the limits prescribed by the moral law and cultured habits.

219

How to put a permanent end to all doubts and questions?

As one advances in spiritual Sadhana and attains a greater and greater degree of evolution day by day, by regular and unremitting practice of the Yoga of Synthesis, the clouds of doubts, delusion and interrogation disperse by themselves. As the sun rises, the mist disappears. Even so, as you progress in the spiritual path by the Grace of Guru and God, all the intricate problems of life and death dissolve themselves into the ever-abiding Truth of existence. The only duty of man is to intensify the inner purity by graded integral Sadhana. Whenever doubts, troubles and the like arise, repeat any one of the following Mantras: *Om Sri Rama Saranam Mama* or *Om Sri Krishna Charanau Saranam*

Prapadye or your Guru Mantra. There is no room for doubts to crop up on the attainment of God-realisation, as the seeker is no longer the seeker, but God Himself.

220

I meditate every now and then on God's glory and omnipotence, but seem to derive no tangible results therefrom. Reasons for it please.

There is no use of praying to the Lord by fits and starts or every now and then. Do Japa and meditation regularly without any break even for a single day. Just as you do not give up tea and meals even for a single day, and just as you do not forget them too, so also, do not leave Sadhana under any circumstance even by way of forgetfulness. First do Sadhana—whatever little you can—and then only take your meals. This is a sure and potent way of goading and compelling the mind to penetrate itself deeply and unavoidably into the spiritual practices. By following this procedure, you get used to doing Sadhana regularly at least for the sake of the meals that is necessarily to succeed, in spite of the unwillingness of the mind.

When the mind undergoes phases of transition in enjoying the charm of the world, it cannot concentrate upon itself and direct the gaze within itself. Pull the reins of the mind back towards itself as it goes out hither and thither. Continue this process several times in a day. When you develop strength of will to realise the Lord by intense efforts, progress automatically sets in. Read the Second Chapter of the Gita with meaning. You will have a clear understanding of the remedy for setbacks in Sadhana.

221

Does it not involve the sin of disobedience if a person becomes a Sadhu disregarding the pious wishes of his parents?

No doubt it helps a person if he takes to Sadhuhood or Sannyasahood with the permission of his parents and other closely related ones; or else, it is likely to affect the interests of the individual. But there is absolutely no harm if he takes to the Nivritti Marga or the path of renunciation when there is a very high degree of Vairagya.

No man in the world is related to any other from the absolute metaphysical standpoint and whatever relationship exists between one and the other is, after all, by dint of Karmas performed previously. Human beings associate and dissociate themselves just as two pieces of wood in a flowing river. When the time ripens, everything resolves itself into One. This makes it clear that one is at liberty to take Sannyas at any desired moment without incurring any inequity, provided one has the staunch Bhav that nobody is related to anybody in this world, and that everybody stands by himself to seek his goal.

222

Do you believe in heaven and hell existing as some independent planes apart from this earth-plane of ours?

Why not? They are also planes of existence just like ours. They are as real as the earthly plane. All the worlds (Lokas) and all the Tirthas (sacred rivers) are existent in the human being himself, if he has belief in the scriptures. One can enjoy heaven or hell in this birth if he so wishes. The greater the grossness, the more intense will be the torture and suffering till such time as the individual is refined and fit for the descent of the Lord's grace by repeated calcinations or purificatory processes.

If you want to enjoy heaven on earth, go on purifying yourself by controlling the lower mind, the desires and cravings. All is bliss, all is joy, all is happiness then. If you allow a free rein to the horses of the senses and yield to the promptings of the devilish mind, if you follow the path of Adharma, hell itself will prevail, not elsewhere in some incredible region, but here on this earth itself.

223

The *Koran* for the Muslims, the *Bible* for the Christians, the *Old Testament* for the Jews, the *Gathas* for the Parsis. What about the Hindus?

The *Gita,* of course. That is the simple, basic scripture for all Hindus. It contains the essence of the Upanishads, gives an optimistic and ideally adequate philosophy of life and shows the main paths of Yoga in an integrated perspective.

224

Since you are an advocate of equality and your teachings do not take into consideration class distinctions, are you in sympathy with communism?

I have nothing to do with politics, much less with any Godless creed. I do not believe that religion or religious teachings should have anything to do with politics. I advocate equal vision in the sense that the

One Reality dwells equally in all beings. Names and forms are changing phenomena. Spirit alone *is*. In a relative sense, the whole humanity is the family of God; there is no high or low in His eyes. As such, a spiritual man's attitude should not be narrowed down by any kind of distinction, be it of class, religion, caste or colour.

225

Is God conscious or unconscious? If He is conscious, He must have a form, for only a being who has a body can be conscious.

God is pure consciousness. He is omniscient, all-knowing. He is Nirakara, formless or incorporeal. This physical body has limited our universal consciousness. Consciousness is of various kinds, viz., physical consciousness, mental consciousness and absolute consciousness. You will experience the highest consciousness when you transcend the three bodies through constant and intense meditation. With this physical body and limited senses you can have the physical consciousness only.

226

If I say, "I am a king", I cannot become a king. So also, if I repeat "Aham Brahma Asmi", I cannot become Brahman.

Besides saying "I am a king", you will have to prepare yourself. You will have to gather a large number of men. You will have to learn many things. You will have to fight. Even so, you will have to prepare and purify the mind. You will have to acquire the four means of salvation—Viveka (discrimination between the real and the unreal), Vairagya (dispassion), Shad Sampat (sixfold virtues) and Mumukshutva (eagerness for liberation). Then you will have to do Sravana (hearing of the Srutis), Manana (reflection) and Nidhidhyasan (constant and profound meditation). Then only you will get Atma Sakshatkara or Brahma Anubhava.

227

If I say, 'Sugar', 'Sugar', I cannot get sugar. If I say 'Ram, Ram', I cannot get God.

You will have to earn money for purchasing sugar. Then you will have to go to the bazaar to purchase sugar. Here also, you will have to get rid of lust, anger, greed, delusion, pride, jealousy and egoism and then repeat 'Ram, Ram' with Bhav (feeling) and single-minded devotion. Then you will have Darshan of Lord Rama. But, Rama is within. Sugar is outside. You will have to give your whole heart to Rama.

228

How to enter Samadhi quickly?

If you want to enter Samadhi quickly, cut off all connections with friends, relatives, etc. Do not write letters to anybody. Observe Akhanda Mouna or the vow of continued silence for one month. Live alone. Walk alone. Take very little but nutritious food; live on milk alone if you can afford. Plunge in deep meditation. Dive deep. Have constant practice. You will be immersed in Samadhi. Be cautious. Use your common sense. Do not make violent struggle with the mind. Relax. Allow the divine thoughts to flow gently in the mind.

229

Why should there be evil?

This is a question which still remains unanswered by sages, Rishis, Acharyas and philosophers. Do not put this question now. You cannot understand it now in your present stage of evolution. It is inexplicable, inscrutable, Anirvachanee Maya. Brahman or God only knows. You will understand it only when you get rid of Maya, when you attain the knowledge of Brahman. This question is put in another way also. Why has God created this universe? Nobody knows the why and how of this universe. Don't rack your brain on this point now. You won't get an answer. You will only waste your energy. Try to go beyond evil. There are ways. Know them and exert.

230

How to get rid of desires?

Develop Viveka or the power of discrimination. Brahman is real. The world is unreal. There is no Vasana or desire in Brahman. The desire is in the mind. Make Vichara. All desires will dwindle into nothing. Mark the Doshas in the objects. The objects are Asat, Jada, Duhkha, impure. Develop burning Mumukshutva. This strong desire for Self-realisation will destroy all other worldly desires. Control the Indriyas also. Develop Vairagya. Give up objects. This is Tyaga. All desires will melt away.

231

If we are tools in the hands of God, are not men free?

Man becomes free only when his individual will becomes merged in the Divine Will. Licentiousness and autocracy must not be mistaken for spiritual freedom. By becoming a tool (Nimitta) in the hands of God, the Bhakta destroys the egoism or the little false 'I', but gains all the Divine Aisvarya or the Siddhis of the Lord. He becomes perfectly free. He has become one with God now.

232

How shall I prepare myself for a contemplative life?

Divide your property between your three sons. Keep something for yourself to keep the life going. Distribute a portion in charity. Build a Kutir in Rishikesh and live there. Don't write letters to your sons. Don't enter into the plains. Then start meditation. Your mind will rest in peace now. Do this at once. You must hurry up.

233

When I was living in Uttarkashi, I had good Nishtha, exalted Vrittis and good Dharma. I have lost them now after entering the plains, even though I do Sadhana. Why? How to raise myself as before?

Contact with worldly-minded people at once affects the mind. Vikshepa comes in. The mind imitates. Bad, luxurious habits are developed. Bad environments and bad associations play a tremendous part and produce a bad influence on the mind of Sadhaks. Old Samskaras are revived. I will ask you to run at once to Uttarkashi, back again. Don't delay even a single minute. As the mind is formed out of the subtlest part of the food, it gets attached to that man from whom it receives its food. Don't be under obligation to anybody. Lead an independent life. Rely on your own self.

234

What is God?

If I give you a good slap on your face, who knows that slap? That knower (Vetta), that knowing subject, is God. When a strong desire is satisfied or gratified, that blissful state wherein the mind finds rest is God. That which sparkles or glitters in your eyes is God. That which prompts you to think is God, the Lord of the mind. The source (Yoni) or support (Adhishthan) for your mind, Prana, senses and body is God.

The tree exists. It shines. It gives delight. These three aspects, existence, shining, delight—Asti-Bhati-Priya or Sat-Chit-Ananda—is God. God is truth. God is love. God is beauty. God is Ananda. God is Light of lights. God is Mind of minds, Prana of Pranas, Soul of souls. That shines in your heart and that is inseparable from you. Feel His presence always. Recognize His presence always, everywhere. Carry His presence when you walk.

235

Why does God create rogues?

As this is a relative world, there must be rogues and honest men. A rogue is not an eternal rogue. A rogue is the saint of the future. Roguery is a negative virtue. It is not a separate entity. Honesty will have no existence in the absence of roguery. The raison d'etre of roguery is to glorify honesty. Roguery and honesty are the obverse and the reverse of the same coin. They are mental creations only. Even a rogue has some virtues. There is neither absolute roguery nor absolute honesty. God Himself plays the part of a rogue in the world's drama for His Lila. There is neither John nor Peter.

236

When I was at Swargashram, your good self told me that we should take eatables from the hands of Mohammedans and should never hesitate from doing so. But our Shastras teach us that we should not accept eatable things from a great sinner. Mohammedans eat beef. Why should we accept any eatable thing from their hands?

If you think that a man is full of vicious deeds, do not take food from his hands. If you think that Lord Siva or Hari dwells even in an evil-minded man, if you entertain this strong idea, you can eat from anybody's hands. Your Drishti or angle of vision is very limited now. You are a beginner in the spiritual line. Your heart is not expanded now. Do plenty of Japa and other religious practices, which I have taught you, wholeheartedly. Feel His indwelling presence in a stone, flower, spoon, towel, in everything. After some time you will be elevated. You will see the Lord only in everything. You have now got a strong anti-Mohammedan Samskara. Destroy it gradually. Love a Mohammedan from the bottom of your heart. Serve him with great devotion. See Hari in his sparkling eyes, in the throbbing of his heart. Have Sattvic Ahara, any kind of pure food. Offer it to God first and then take it as Prasada or sacrament. Repeat His Name before you take food. Thus you can purify or spiritualize any kind of impure food.

237

Yoga practice, they say, is meant only for men, because it is they who require control. I wonder what work is assigned to women, then! Sit at home and breed children, I presume! But, is it a fact that only men need the Yoga practice? Can women not become great Yoginis in the same way as men become great Yogis? Or, does it depend on the sex also? Why has sex stood between women and spiritual greatness?

Queen Chudalai was a great Yogini. She had many higher Siddhis. She even converted her husband Sikhidhvaja and helped him in his salvation. Read the story of Chudalai in Yoga Vasishtha. Ladies lack in Vairagya and in the power of endurance. They have not got the same faculties as men have. Hence many Yoginis do not crop up amongst ladies. Ladies can have Darshan of the Lord easily as they have ingrained devotion in them, as the element of Sneha or love is predominant in them. Sex is no bar to spiritual greatness. Gargi, Madalasa and Sulabha were all reputed Yoginis.

238

How does a Jnani look into the objects? Describe his vision.

This is indescribable. This is one's feeling. Sometimes when you sleep, you scratch the body and drive off flies. If anybody asks you, "Do you remember the scratching, the driving off of flies, when you were asleep?", you will say, "No". Similarly, even though a

Jnani sees, he does not see. He is always conscious of his Svarupa. If he likes, he can have a double consciousness and turn his vision that side and this side also. His activities are like those of children. Owing to the mental retentum—the force of the old Subha Vasanas and the Lesha Avidya or trace of ignorance—, his activities are kept up. Just as the tin in which asafoetida or garlic had been kept emits the smell of these drugs even though the tin is washed several times with soap and water, this trace of Avidya remains in the Jivanmukta till Prarabdha wears away. He is not doing actions at all from his own viewpoint. The bystanders think that the Jnani also is working. But we have to admit that there is Lesha Avidya or a trace of ignorance, because we notice that the Jnani also eats, bathes and answers calls of nature.

239

You have said in one of your lessons that the aspirant should fast only once a month. But Gandhiji and others have stressed the importance of fasting. They say that one should fast at least three or four times in a month. Moreover, they point out that fasting helps self-control. How is it that you do not allow frequent fasting?

Fasting does help in self-control. But, too much fasting weakens the body and the mind and retards spiritual Sadhana. I am also a strong votary of fasting. Fasting is a great Prayaschitta. It expiates any kind of sin quickly. It has got a tremendous purifying influence on the heart. Read Manu Smriti. As the vast majority are afraid of fasting too much, I have prescribed only a day of fasting in a month. Young, robust, plethoric people can fast twice or thrice in a month if passion troubles them much.

240

I am a theist. Why is it that I become an atheist sometimes when I mix with materialistic people?

Your spiritual Samskaras are not yet strong. You are not yet moulded properly. You need Satsang for one year more. You should repeat 200 Malas of any Mantra daily (200 x 108 = 21,600 times). You should take Sattvic food only, such as rice, Dhal, bread, fruits and milk. Give up meat at once. Observe Mouna for two hours daily. Live alone for two hours in a room. Introspect. Meditate. Watch your thoughts carefully.

241

Will there be continuity of consciousness during suspension of breath? Kindly explain to me with an illustration.

Hari Singh was a Hatha Yogi. He was buried underneath the ground in a box for three months in Ranjit Singh's court. He came back with life when the box was opened. Hatha Yogis block the Talu Chakra, the posterior nasal openings, with their elongated tongue that is obtained through Bahir Kechari Mudra Kriya of Chalan (moving the tongue frequently), Doshan (dragging the tongue with butter) and Chedan (cutting the *frenulum lingua* that is underneath the tongue). They drink slowly the nectar that dribbles from the Sahasrara Chakra through the opening in the palate. This instance of Hari Singh clearly indicates that the real "I" is entirely distinct from Prana. In spite of the suspension of breath, Hari Singh had continuity of consciousness.

242

It takes a long time to remove Mala and Vikshepa. What to do?

If you want to become a Master of Arts, it takes a large number of years. You will have to pass through the Matriculation, Intermediate and B.A. courses and then take up the M.A. course. Even so, you will have to plod on and persevere for many years to remove the Mala and the Vikshepa. How patiently does the fisherman wait with concentrated gaze to catch a single fish! When such is the case for a trifling thing, what to speak of attaining Brahma-Jnana? It is *Kshurasya Dhara,* walking along the blade of a sharp razor.

243

A Vritti arises: "Let me renounce the world and do Bhajan in a secluded place like Rishikesh". Immediately another Vritti arises: "Let me remain as a Grihastha and practise Yoga like Janaka". How can I know, Swamiji, whether this particular Vritti comes from the Atma or the mind or the Buddhi? I am perplexed.

An ordinary worldly-minded man can hardly hear the inner voice of Atma. He cannot get pure thoughts of Vichara also. Any Sattvic thought emanates from the Sattvic Buddhi. In the case of worldlings, all thoughts emanate from the mind only. He who does Nishkama Karma Yoga and has purity of mind begins to entertain thoughts of God. Generally the mind raises various sorts of curious, fantastic thoughts. It deludes all. It may pretend to do Vichar. When it comes to practicality, it will do nothing. If there is serious determination in you to concentrate and meditate, and if you put it into actual practice for months steadily, and if the longing for the Darshan of God or Self-realisation becomes keen and acute, then alone think that all these kinds of thoughts proceed from your Sattvic Buddhi only.

244

Can you please give me some detailed practical hints to get non-attachment in mind in our every action?

Think that you are an instrument (Nimitta) in the hands of God when you work. Egoism and respectability will vanish. Don't expect fruits for your actions (Nishkamya). How can you expect fruits when another, viz., God, is working through you? Further, when you are aware that the world is full of miseries, what is the use of coming back again into the world ? You are a toy in the hands of God. He holds the string. He is the Sutradhar. Do all actions from a sense of duty. Reduce your wants. Lead a very simple life. Hate luxury. Control the Indriyas. Look at everyone and everything in the world as the manifestation of Narayana. Think that this world is illusory and a long dream. How can there be attachment now in the mind, my dear Ramachandra? If you do actions in this way, you will become a practical Yogi. I assure you. Cheer your spirit. Gird up the loins and engage yourself boldly in the daily battle of life.

245

Why should God drive me to do a bad action?

God never drives you to do any bad action. He is always the Sakshi or witness. Your own nature, your own evil Samskaras, force you to do actions. *"Svabhavastu Pravartate"* says the Gita (Ch. V-14). You lack in Viveka or discrimination. That is the reason why you become a slave of passion. God has given you Buddhi to check passion. Why don't you use it then?

246

I never intend to do any evil action. Is it my responsibility when I do it? If it is, will God forgive me? If He forgives me, what about the fruit of that action? I write to you candidly, for I have chosen you to be my noble guide. Please forgive me and help me.

You are certainly responsible for the action. God never forgives. Action brings on its own fruits. Through Prayaschitta or expiatory rites you can destroy the evil effects of a bad action. You actually suffer in Prayaschitta. Hence the evil effects are washed off. The evil Karma will not follow you to the next birth. Sincere repentance, Japa, fasting and charity can destroy the evil effects of bad Karma. In repentance you actually suffer. This serves to wash off the evil effects of the bad action. Repentance must be done with a contrite heart. You must not repeat the evil action again.

247

Why do different prophets give contradictory teachings?

Prophets are born from time to time to remove a catastrophe and establish Dharma. They preach according to the time, place, conditions and requirements. Lord

Buddha preached, "Don't kill". Guru Govind Singh preached, "Kill". When Buddha was born, people were sacrificing many animals. He had to preach Ahimsa to stop killing. Guru Govind Singh had to infuse chivalry in man. One prophet preached, "Renounce and go to the forest". Sri Ramanuja preached, "Enjoy at home. Have no attachment. Worship Vishnu". The teachings are not contradictory in reality. They are needed to suit the occasion, time and nature of men.

248

Why has God created some souls in a pure state and others in a state of cruelty? Why does He make some do bad acts and prevent their becoming good? When can I have perfection?

You can have perfection and immortality through long struggle. The mortal in the relative plane does good and evil acts. Evil also is a negative good. Out of evil, sometimes good cometh. Everyone learns lessons in this world and evolves. God is only a witness. He does not make men do evil acts. Man has intellect and free will. Man, out of his egoism, does actions according to his own sweet will and reaps the fruits of evil actions. When the Sattvic material or purity increases by practising virtuous actions, he becomes divine. God is not responsible.

249

You say that forgiveness should be practised. Being not the final authority in my office, I cannot save my subordinates from getting punished. If I conceal their offences or mistakes, I will not be doing my duty

properly and this may one day get me into trouble. When I forward the reports of my subordinates, they are punished and I feel sorry for it. What should I do in such cases?

You can forgive the minor mistakes of your servants and subordinates. This cannot bring in any trouble. Keep your conscience clean. Warn them whenever they commit mistakes. As you are in the Vyavaharic field, you will have to punish those who commit serious mistakes. But, be unbiased. Have fear of God. If poor servants are fined, give them some money from your own pocket. Love them. They will not commit mistakes in future.

250

May I enquire how the power of concentration increases?

Concentration increases by curtailing your wants and desires, by observing Mouna for two hours daily, by remaining in seclusion in a quiet room for one or two hours daily, by practising Pranayam, by prayer, by increasing the number of sittings in meditation in the evening and at night, by Vichar, etc.

251

How is it possible that a Creator, so full of love, created a world and a nature where animals can live only by killing other animals that have to endure terrible pain and suffering? Nobody can give me a satisfactory answer.

If men kill each other, it is sin; they *need not*. But, animals cannot live without killing the other animals for food. What do you say? We are anxious for your opinion.

God's love for the created universe knows no bounds; He cannot be held responsible for the experiences of created beings. God does not punish or reward anyone in a personal way; it is one's own actions, sinful or good, that works as the cause of experience here.

As the human being is endowed with moral sense and as he is invested with the consciousness of doership and responsibility, he imposes this sense of morality and responsibility of action on sub-human beings also. The defect, therefore, lies in man and not in the animals which act without any consciousness of ethical conduct, and spontaneously, free from the responsibility connected with doership or agency.

No action can produce a retributive effect unless it is done with the consciousness of personal doership and responsibility. Man shall be punished by retributive justice, for man has the freedom to act and he is responsible for what he does. But animals have not been endowed with such a freedom and power of understanding and reason; so what they do is just the expression of the instinctive natural promptings in them and this is included in the scheme of the universal nature. Nature is beyond moral laws. Moral conduct is only for man, meant to restrict his behaviour and lead him on to universal consciousness through gradual ascent along the evolutionary ladder.

All things born must die. And there should be some immediate cause for the destruction of things. This cause of destruction may be another animal, an earthquake, a thunder-stroke, flood, disease, storm or any such thing. These should not be clothed with moral and ethical values except when these are connected with human agency.

252

Sometimes I hush up things in my mind. I get mental torments thereby. What shall I do to get rid of this habit?

You must be frank and as simple as a child. Then only you will get the divine light. You will grow spiritually. Even if it is a horrible crime, you must admit it before a Guru. Then only you will get his sympathy and protection. By admitting your faults before others, you remove the effects of bad actions. It serves as a Prayaschitta or expiatory action.

253

What are the advantages of Mouna or the vow of silence? Should I also observe?

Observe Mouna for a couple of hours daily at any time that suits you. Try to speak little at other times. Avoid unnecessary conversations. Don't talk harsh words and obscene language. Talk sweetly and gently. You must have perfect control over speech. Control over speech means control of mind. The organ of speech, Vak Indriya, is a great distractor of the mind. Mouna gives you peace. It removes anxieties and quarrels. It develops your will power. It conserves energy. It reduces the force of Sankalpa or the thought-current.

254

Will a Jivanmukta also take birth?

Some Jivanmuktas whose hearts are filled with mercy and Vyavahar Apeksha for Lokasangraha like the Buddhistic Arhats may, out of their own free will, take a birth—like Sri Sankara, Sri Dattatreya or Jnana Dev. They need not do any Sadhana as they are born Siddhas. At once they appear as spiritual luminaries, do some spiritual preaching, write out some precious philosophical books, set aright some catastrophe, pass off quickly and merge in Brahman (Videha Kaivalyam). They are all Amsa-Avataras with special Isvara Kala (spiritual rays).

255

God-realised souls, on leaving the mortal coil, merge in the cosmos and thus do not have any individuality on any plane. However, it is claimed that saints like Sai Baba and others, who have attained Moksha, do help and guide those devotees who seek their blessings. How can we explain this apparent contradiction?

Realised souls, who wish to help the devotees even after they give up their physical bodies, retain their astral bodies (Sukshma Sarira) for the sake of their eagerness to help those that are in need of their help. But Jivanmuktas, generally, do not retain their astral bodies just in order to help the aspirants, since there will always be highly evolved souls on the relative plane, who will carry on the task of teaching the spiritual aspirants.

256

At times I feel that I am entrapped in Maya and try to extricate myself. At other times I feel that I am the Atma which is changeless and pure. I am looking for your Kripa which will certainly take me out of this ocean of troubles. Any instructions?

You are in the struggling stage. You are doubtless progressing. You will soon be established in your real Svarup. Fear not. Plod on. Persevere. Don't look back. March on boldly. The goal is very near. Be a Sakshi of all your actions. You are Asanga, Akarta (unattached, non-doer). Thou art that Immortal Atma!

257

I am having spiritual practice for the last three years. I do not find any improvement. Why?

There is improvement. Your mental images are strong and steady now. Remember that there is no barometer or thermometer to read your spiritual progress in the spiritual realm. You are now giving only half of your mind to God. Collect the dissipated rays and give the full mind to God. I assure you, "You will realise Him this very moment".

258

Difficulties and anxieties upset me in every way. Failure and troubles face me on every side. Domestic duties trouble my Sadhan. What shall I do, my Lord?

Don't be afraid. Remember the saying, "Even this will pass away". Write this on a piece of paper in bold types and fix it on the wall in your room. Difficulties and troubles are Agamapaya. They come and go. Read Verse 14 in Chapter 2 of Srimad Bhagavad Gita. Become a hero. Stand firm as a rock. Live in the Centre. Live in Om. Live in Truth or Atma. Nothing can shake you. Difficulties will make you more strong and endow you with more endurance. Mysterious are His ways. Say, "Thy will be done".

259

How is it that we see many wicked persons flourishing in this world while the good souls suffer? Why is God merciful to some and heartless to some else?

This is an age-old question, as old as the world itself. The great Bhishma shed tears when he was on his death-bed. When questioned why he cried, he replied that the Pandavas were great devotees of the Lord and always abided by the laws of Dharma. Above all, the Lord was constantly with them in the form of Krishna. And yet they underwent so much of suffering.

Some wicked persons do flourish in this world of hypocrisy, but it does not mean that they are free from suffering. The really good souls do not suffer as much as the 'flourishing' wicked ones, for peace is in the hearts of the former. To be able to abide by the ideals they hold sacred is by itself a great cause of happiness. The welfare and the misery of people can be explained only in terms of the law of Karma.

Good persons suffer because of the mistakes they had committed in their past incarnations. Wicked persons, who seem to be well off, are now reaping the results of their past good actions, but will have to pay the price of their present ones, later. It is the law of Karma that lifts God above all the good and the bad conditions of man. If God were made responsible for the material state of affairs of the individual or the enjoyment or suffering of man, then God would cease to be God, for a partial God, dishing out favours to some and withholding them from the others, would be no God at all.

260

What is the feeling of a Jnani when he eats a mango or some delicious food?

He has not the idea of Bhokta, Bhoga and Bhogya (enjoyer, enjoyment and enjoyable). The eating of a mango will not produce any Samskara in him. He will not think again at a certain time, "I ate a delicious mango at Mr. Raman's bungalow last year". He has not the Kama Sankalpa. He is free from the Bhav, "Aham Bhokta" or "I am enjoyer". He is aware of the hunger. He is aware that hunger is the Dharma of the Pranamaya Kosha and that something or the other should be thrust inside the stomach to appease this hunger.

261

Can you, at a distance half across the earth, intuit the nature of my life-mission?

Your life-mission is absolute dedication of all your faculties to the Lord, and not to be *curious* to know how He is to make use of you. It is not for nothing that He has hidden from our view His higher purposes. Our little mind cannot reason out the meanings of events which He brings to pass. So He does not take off the veil nor need we be curious to know. Surrender yourself to Him completely. He has already chosen you and He will give you commissions from time to time. Carry them out unselfishly and rise up higher and higher in Divine service. That will be the true expression, in thought and deed, of your love for God and His creation, the world.

262

Is it true that death (voluntary or otherwise) places us in a more conducive environment in the next birth for the fulfilment of certain deep-rooted desires which are otherwise difficult to fulfil in this life?

Death need not necessarily place one in a more conducive environment in the next birth. That depends upon the quality of man's actions during the present birth as well as in the remoter past. It is true that our desires guide our future births to a great extent.

263

Which among the Yogic Asans will help a married lady to keep her youth for a considerable period?

Sarvangasan, Matsyasan, Sirshasan, Padahastasan, Halasan, Paschimottanasan and Chakrasan, coupled with Yoga Mudra and Viparitakarani Mudra, help quite a lot to keep up bodily poise and tension. All these need not necessarily be taken up simultaneously. Whichever of these are found convenient can be practised, along with Pranayam, within the boundary limits of health and not overriding the limitations of her sex. A lover of Yoga—male or female—should have restricted carnal desires.

264
Why do the Hindus give more importance to the Bhagavad Gita than to the Uttara Gita?

The Bhagavad Gita is more comprehensive and detailed in the exposition of the philosophy and teachings of Sri Krishna. Rather, it is a *magnum opus* among the scriptures of the Hindus, and so, in substance and scope, it is more important than the Uttara Gita, also of Sri Krishna. But please note that there are many Gitas, such as the Anu Gita, Avadhuta Gita and so on, all of which are helpful to the spiritual aspirant. Yet, among all the Gitas—quite a few dozens of them, major and minor—, the Bhagavad Gita is the most important, integral, comprehensive and the best.

265
I understand the biggest mistake an aspirant often makes is to falsely identify lower Samadhi with higher or the highest Samadhi; but, how can a man who makes such a mistake guard himself against it?

When one rises to the state of Samadhi, he does not make the mistake of doubting as to whether it is lower or higher or the highest. He knows what it is without doubt, quite naturally.

266
What are the marks of spiritual progress? How can one know whether he is advanced in the spiritual path or not?

Peace, cheerfulness, contentment, dispassion, fearlessness and an unperturbed state of mind under all conditions indicate that you are advancing in the spiritual path.

Spiritual progress is not measured by Siddhis or powers, but only by the depth of your bliss in meditation.

These are the sure tests of your spiritual progress:—

Is your interest in inner spiritual activity and outer Sadhana increasing day after day?

Does spiritual life mean to your consciousness a matter of great delight, a delight far transcending the happiness that the world of vital pleasures affords you or offers you?

Has your personal awareness come to a possession of a sense of peace and strength which men who are not aspirants do not find in their everyday lives?

Do you feel certain that your power of discrimination and light of thought have been steadily growing?

Is your life being gradually led to such experiences which reveal to you the operation of a will and intelligence other than your own, the will and intelligence of the Omnipotent Lord?

Has there come into the conscious activities of your everyday life, the active function of a new delightful angle of vision, a new perspective, a strong sense of self-possession, a steadily growing conviction of your dependence upon and intimate relation with the all-pervading Divinity?

If your answers to all these questions or to any one of them are in the affirmative, be absolutely sure that you are progressing, and progressing speedily, in the spiritual path.

267

When the Jiva undergoes transmigration and takes another birth after leaving this physical body, is it necessary that we should perform the Shraddha ceremony for him? He is no more in the heavens. To whom will the oblations go?

The Pitris remain in heaven, Pitri Loka or Chandra Loka, for a very long period. The enjoyments in heaven and the peace of the departed soul are enhanced by the performance of the Shraddha ceremony. Likewise, the sufferings of the departed soul in worlds other than heaven are mitigated by the performance of the Shraddha ceremony by his sons. Thus, in both cases, the performance of Shraddha is a great help.

And even if the individual takes another birth immediately after his death, as happens in rare cases, the performance of Shraddha adds to his happiness in his new birth. So, it is the imperative duty of everybody to perform the Shraddha ceremony for his parents and forefathers. The Shraddha ceremony should be performed with great Sraddha or faith as long as you live. Faith is the main support for religion.

The various religious observances imposed upon mankind by the Shastras tend to purify the ignorant man. The Shraddha ceremony, being one of the obligatory duties as per the injunctions of the scriptures, also tends to purify the mind. Besides this, the forefathers are also pleased and their good wishes and blessings tend to our material and spiritual growth.

268

How long should one practise Sirshasan or Paschimottanasan or Kumbhak or Maha Mudra to awaken the Kundalini? Nothing is mentioned on this point in any book on Yoga.

It all depends upon the degree of purity, stage of evolution, the degree of purification of the Nadis and the Pranamaya Kosha, and the degree of Vairagya and yearning for liberation.

A student starts his Sadhana from the point or stage he left in his previous birth. Some are born with purity and other requisites of realisation on account of their having undergone the necessary discipline in their past life. They are born Siddhas. Guru Nanak, Jnana Dev of Alandi, Vama Dev and Ashtavakra were all adepts from their very boyhood. Guru Nanak, when he was a boy, asked his teacher in the school about the significance of OM. Vama Dev delivered lectures on Vedanta when he was dwelling in his mother's womb.

269

I am a devotee of Lord Siva. Should I go to temples dedicated to Lord Vishnu or Devi also? And if I go, how shall I worship the Deities there?

Yes, you should never miss an opportunity of visiting and worshipping at any shrine you come across. When you go to a temple of Lord Vishnu or Devi, worship Lord Siva Himself there. Look upon the Deity in the temple as another form of Lord Siva. If your father came to you in the attire of a High Court Judge, or being an actor in a drama, if he came to you in the dress of a female, will you turn away from him? You will greet him as your own father in any case. Similar should be your attitude in worshipping the Lord. God is one. He is worshipped and adored variously by various people.

270

Swamiji, what is the sense in worshipping the Guru as people do here in India? Isn't that slavery? You mean to say that the disciple becomes the slave of the Guru?

Aren't you grateful to the man who serves you and helps you? Don't you express your gratitude to him in some form or the other? If you behave that way with a man who has helped you a little bit in a secular way, how much more ought to be your gratitude to the man who shows you the path to the Supreme? He has given you new life, nay, immortality and eternal bliss. Can you refrain from expressing your gratitude to him? Actual worship of the Guru is the Indian way of expressing this highest gratitude. You express gratitude to the man who has helped you by giving him something; and to the Guru—the man who has bestowed upon you the highest gift of spiritual knowledge—you give yourself!

That is not slavery. Oh, no. The real Guru can never enslave the aspirant. In fact, the real Guru is the seeker's servant! The real Guru has the highest kind of love for the aspirant. The Guru is in his heart; the Guru has won the disciple's heart; the two have become one now. There will be divine love between the two—not slavery.

271

How can a person, who has been thinking in a negative way for a long time, change to positive thinking?

Let him start with some positive suggestive formulas: "I am hale and hearty. I am healthy. There is nothing wrong with me. I was under a misconception of my own abilities and capacities. Now I have realised my real nature". Let him do it with the help of some person advanced in Yoga or a devotee of the Lord. Let him start with a prayer to the Lord. Let him make prayer a part of his daily life and 'a must' in life. All negative thinking will end and he will become quite normal.

272

What is the purpose of singing Kirtans constantly?

Singing of Kirtans incessantly will produce divine vibrations within and these vibrations are so powerful as to counteract all external forces distracting the human mind and arrest the wanderings of the mind, bringing peace and happiness to the individual. There is a mysterious power in the Divine Name that singing it purifies the heart and mind and makes the Kirtanist God-conscious.

SUBJECT INDEX
(Figures indicate Question Numbers)

A

Advaita and Saguna Bhakti	123
Akashvani	143
Arjuna	210
Asceticism	148
rationale of	139
Astral body	100
Ayurveda	47

B

Beauty	217
Bhagavad Gita	223
fact or fiction	42
and the rationale of creation	81
locale for the teaching of the	92
Bhakti	
vis-a-vis Jnana	13, 14
how to develop	156
Brahmacharya	
Sirshasana and	13
failure in	16
family life and	181, 188, 207
Brahmamuhurta	
glory of	3

C

Chitta Suddhi	
signs to indicate	172

Cinema	218
Communism	224
Concentration	
easy way to	174
how to increase the power of	250
Conscience	208
on the killing of	205
Consciousness	225
cosmic	136
continuity of	241
Contentment	
and defeatist mentality	38
idleness and	121
Cow-slaughter	142
Creation	
the 'why' of	23, 32, 78

D

Dance	151
Death	99, 149
Deer-skin	89
Desire	126, 230
Devotion	
how to develop	132

E

Earth	150
Ethics	

and the Industrial
  Revolution 33
Evil 229, 248

F

Fasting 177
  frequency in 239
Food
  vegetarian and
  non-vegetarian 28

G

Gandhiji
  assassination of 82
  politics and 152
Ganges, sacredness of 8, 234
God
  belief in 1, 2
God-realisation
  married life and 192
Goodness 84
  vis-a-vis saintliness 114
Grace
  how to invoke 6
  manifestations of 31
  difficulties and 86
Greatness
  criteria for measuring 35
Guru 179
  necessity for a 49
  on changing the 66, 75
  qualifications of a 87
  worship of the 270

H

Hatha Yoga
  age and 171
Heaven 222

Hell 222

I

Idol worship 190
  Ikons 58
Indigestion
  removal of 140
Ishta Devata 112

J

Jesus 58
Jiva
  evolution of the 34
Jivanmukta 254
  astral body of a 255
Jnani
  vision of a 238, 260

K

Kala
  meaning of 135
Karma
  how to free oneself
  from 137
Karma Yoga
  practice of 182
Kevala Kumbhak 63
Kirtan
  purpose of 272
Krishna
  and His play with the
  Gopis 102
Kundalini
  Japa and 10
  ascent of 72
  awakening of 133

L

Life 149
  goal of 129, 261
Lust
  conquest of 141

M

Mahavakyas
  significance of the 116
Mary 58
Maya
  origin of 120
Meat-eating 202
Meditation
  distinguished from Japa 5
  advisability after night meal 15
  life and 111
  clues to success in 128
Mediumship 105
Mind 154
  faults in the 11
  purification of the 12
  how to control the 48, 168
  higher and lower 56
  distinguished from soul 88
Moha
  power of 109
  conquest of 166
Moksha
  need for 113
Mouna 253
Music 151
  power of 163

N

Nadi Suddhi
  indications of 39

Naga Sadhus 201
National character 79
Nauli 117
Nirguna Brahman
  meaning of 134
Nirvikalpa Samadhi 60

P

Pada Puja 214
Philosopher
  and the man of the world 119
Pilgrimage
  vis-a-vis a sight-seeing trip 20
  benefits of a 21
Politics
  vis-a-vis religion 161
Pranayama 90, 203
  and the need for a Guru 27
  and its suitability for women 91
  obstructed breathing and 96
Prarabdha
  power of 24
  how to overcome 45
Prayers
  miracles and 65
Preordination
  and free will 108, 157

R

Rama
  grief of 103
Ram Tirth 167
Realised soul
  how to know a 17

Reason
  limitations of 46
Rebirth 52, 53
  interval before 54
  desires and 211
  immediate 162
  world population and 176
Religion
  economic betterment
    and 106
Retributive justice 164
Rogues 235

S

Sadasiva Brahmendra 2, 194
Sadhana 257
  and city life 51
  signs of progress in 122
  regularity in 220
  obstacles to 258
Sadhus
  begging and 118
Saints 59, 195
  curses of 30
Samadhi
  how to enter into 228
Sannyasa
  test of one's fitness
    for 22, 95
  vis-a-vis family life 29
  seclusion and 94
  and the need for
    progeny 98
  worldly connections
    and 159
  family responsibilities
    and 130, 167
  coloured cloth and 180

how to qualify for 186
and parents' permission 221
Sannyasins
  and their contributions
    to society 101
Sanskrit 183
Scriptures 209
  study of 178
Seance 104
Self, nature of the 83
Semen 196
Senses
  abstraction of the 125
Serenity
  how to develop 199
Service
  scope for 131
Sex energy
  sublimation of the 43
Sex urge 216
Shraddha
  the importance of 267
Sin
  procreation and 206
Sirshasana 203
Siva Linga
  esoteric meaning
    of the 173
Sleep
  control of 68
Smoking
  how to stop 80
Social work 198
Soul
  proof for the existence
    of the 7
Spiritual literature
  value of 61, 62

Suffering
of virtuous
men 70, 155, 259
Suicide 153, 197
Superconsciousness 127

T

Thought-reading 74
Tiger-skin 89
Truth
inviolability of 44

U

Universe
evolution of the 73
Untouchability 71

V

Vibrations
spiritual 124, 165

W

Women 160
and spiritual life 26
devotional nature of 144
role of 191
and Yoga practice 237
World
nature of its unreality 187
World peace
role of politicians in 85

Y

Yogasanas
women and 9, 204
Yogi
and reaction to disease 41
powers of a 158
Yogic vision
nature of 107